DATE DUE

MR 26 '97	OC 24 '02		
RENEW	NO 25 '02		
AP 30 '97	OC 31 03		
JE 27 '97	FE 11 '04		
DE 19 '97	JE 6 '07		
MY 28 '98			
OC 26 '98			
DE 15 '98			
AP 20 '99			
MY 20 99			
AU 25 '00			
MY 24 '00			
JA 22 '01			
JE 7 '01			
NO 2 '01			

DEMCO 38-296

The Iraqi Invasion of Kuwait

The Iraqi Invasion of Kuwait
Saddam Hussein, His State and International Power Politics

MUSALLAM ALI MUSALLAM

British Academic Press
LONDON · NEW YORK

Published in 1996 by
British Academic Press
an imprint of I.B.Tauris & Co Ltd
45 Bloomsbury Square
London WC1A 2HY

A full CIP record for this book is available from the British Library

ISBN 1 86064 020 6

Typeset in Monotype Baskerville
by Philip Armstrong, Sheffield

Printed and bound in Great Britain by
WBC Ltd, Bridgend, Mid Glamorgan

To Ali bin Musallam, my beloved father and friend, whose wisdom, advice and example shall remain with me all the days of my life.

Contents

Acknowledgements

I am grateful first and foremost, to each of the Georgetown University faculty members who so kindly served on my Dissertation Committee: Professor Robert J. Lieber, Chairman; Professor William V. O'Brien; and Professor Ibrahim Ibrahim.

Professor Lieber, Chairman of the Department of Government, gave generously of his time and ideas to advise and encourage me throughout my academic career at Georgetown. Professor O'Brien, a leading expert on international law, helped me explore and develop my academic interests, drawing on his own lengthy and illustrious career. Professor Ibrahim, a renowned authority on the Arab world in general and the Gulf region in particular, guided me through the intellectual labyrinth of Middle East politics as my professor and friend.

I am deeply indebted also to all the members of my family for their unfailing love and encouragement, in good times and in bad, during the years of my work. My most heartfelt thanks go to my wife, Sara, for the strength of her love and support across so many miles, and to my mother, for her boundless love and belief in me.

Finally, I am fortunate to have had the blessing of many good friends who helped along the way with warm words, constructive ideas and critical perspectives, all of which proved invaluable to me. I am especially grateful to Mary McDavid, who helped immensely with her editorial acumen and critical advice.

Introduction

Iraq's invasion of Kuwait initiated one of the most important international conflicts since the Second World War. Yet it is also one of the least well understood in terms of its causes, its immediate outcome and its likely long-term effects on the politics of the region. Not only was it unprecedented for a member-state of the United Nations to invade and annex another member, it was also anomalous, within the framework of Arab politics, for a member-state of the League of Arab States to force a neighbouring state to relinquish its national sovereignty. Moreover, the challenge posed to the international order by the invasion prompted a novel response: the creation of a successful diplomatic and military coalition comprised of 33 countries – a phenomenon of unity, organisation, and military–political cohesiveness without parallel in post-Second World War international affairs. This achievement required an intricate and unique consensus among the coalition members, marked by the mobilisation of well over half a million multinational troops, and a formidable assemblage of the most advanced high-technology conventional weaponry the world has ever known.

As in the case of most wars, Iraq's march into Kuwait, once it occurred, developed its own momentum. In hindsight, some would argue that it was inevitable. However, the war was neither sudden in conception nor simple in execution, despite some experts' political assessments. Furthermore, despite the decisive victory of the allies and the expulsion of all Iraqi forces from Kuwait, no clear explanation for Iraq's audacious act of war has emerged as of this writing.

One approach to an understanding of the causes of the war would be to treat it as the culmination of a chain of events which, some might argue, made war inevitable.[1] As with many such chains, the first link is difficult to identify.[2] From one historical perspective, the starting point might be found in the aftermath of the First World War when Britain established the current borders of the region. In October 1932,

Iraq became a sovereign state when the British mandate from the League of Nations ended. Britain, however, stayed on in neighbouring Kuwait until 1961, when her withdrawal triggered the first major Gulf crisis of the post-colonial era in the Middle East: Iraq refused to recognise Kuwait's independence and laid claim to large areas of Kuwaiti territory, moving troops to Basra, the Iraqi city closest to the Kuwaiti border. On that occasion Britain supported Kuwait, and the Arab world united against Iraqi claims and proved its strong resolve by sending substantial forces to Kuwait, including a deployment of 10,000 Egyptian soldiers. The British delayed their final departure until the Arab forces had arrived, at which point Baghdad conceded the issue and backed down, for the moment.

The next turning point – one which seems to have driven Iraq to become more of a military state – came in 1975 when a long-simmering dispute with Iran over the sovereignty of the Shatt al-Arab waterway to the Gulf burst into the open. Iran, with three times Iraq's population and much stronger militarily, had for years been arming Kurds within Iraqi territory. An insurgency in the northern part of Iraq, supported by Iran, created the prospect (or illusion) of a separate, oil-rich Kirkuk, administered by its majority Kurdish inhabitants. After much diplomatic manoeuvring between the two states the Treaty of Algiers was signed in 1975, providing for a discontinuation of Iranian support for the Kurds, but ceding Iranian claims to the Shatt al-Arab strait, landlocked Iraq's only access to the Persian Gulf. Saddam Hussein later claimed the treaty was the result of coercion, and this unresolved border issue came back to haunt the region, as one of the causes of the bloody and protracted Iran–Iraq War of 1980–88. Apart from this, the principal Iranian diplomatic triumph – one that would cast a long and bitter shadow – was to humiliate the Iraqi prime minister, then Saddam Hussein, by compelling him to expel the Iranian dissident religious leader, Ayatollah Khomeini, from Iraq, where he had sought refuge.

The Iran–Iraq war of 1980–88 was in its turn a watershed on the road to the 1990 war. The conflict between Iran and Iraq entered a new phase after the stunning success of the Islamic revolution in Iran in 1979. A militarily powerful but stable and predictable Iran was replaced by an openly hostile and belligerent Islamic government in Tehran, headed by the Ayatollah Khomeini. Iran experienced political chaos and faced a bleak, uncertain future. The political star of Saddam

Hussein, on the other hand, had ascended to the point that he was the absolute and unassailable ruler of Iraq. Moreover, Iraq was by this time wealthy enough to gain easy access to some of the most sophisticated military equipment the world's armaments manufacturers could offer. Exploiting the opportunity offered by this sudden change in the balance of power with Iran and simultaneously fearing that Shi'a fundamentalism might threaten the state, as the Iranian government attempted to mobilise Iraq's Shi'a community toward an Islamic revolution, Saddam Hussein set about righting the Treaty of Algiers.

In 1980 Saddam decided upon a pre-emptive attack against Iran and sent his army into the southern territories of his neighbour. The subsequent war continued for eight long years, claiming more than a million lives on both sides. It destroyed Iraq's newly built infrastructure, exhausted its oil reserve wealth, involved the country in a foreign debt of approximately $80 billion, and eventually even led to Iraq's concession of some of its territory.

Although the two nations arrived at a cease-fire agreement in August 1988, when Ayatollah Khomeini accepted UN resolution 598, the Iraqi government was soon to discover that this was far from the end of the episode. Not only was the country burdened with a huge military machine it could ill afford, with approximately a million men under arms, but its domestic population was beginning to ask awkward questions: to what end had they made so many terrible and staggering sacrifices? What was to be their reward? There seemed to be no satisfactory answer.

Two years later, still faced with this political dilemma, the Iraqi government resorted to drastic measures. During the war Iraq had run up huge debts as a result of loans made by neighbouring Arab nations. Its Arab allies refused to write these loans off and, needing an external enemy as a scapegoat for popular resentment, Iraq turned on its former friends in the Gulf. Kuwait in particular was accused not only of ignoring Iraqi sacrifices by refusing to forgive its neighbour's debt, but also of actually using the war situation to its own advantage. Kuwait and the United Arab Emirates (UAE) were, according to Iraq, producing more oil than their OPEC quotas allowed, thus lowering prices. In July 1990, Saddam Hussein threw down the gauntlet, accusing Kuwait of costing Iraq over $1 billion a month in oil revenues and waging economic war against Iraq.

The Kuwaiti ruling family was aware of Iraq's increasingly desperate situation and in an attempt to avert a military disaster, offered Iraq a compromise. It would provide $500 million in immediate aid, and lease to Iraq for some 90 years the islands necessary to give Baghdad access to the sea because the Shatt al-Arab was blocked by sunken ships from the Iran–Iraq war strewn about the waterway. Furthermore, although for reasons of accounting it would not formally forgive the Iraqi war debt, the Kuwaiti government promised not to insist upon prompt repayment.

For Saddam Hussein, however, these offers were not sufficient and Iraqi troops were massed on the Kuwaiti border. Few Arab governments actually expected Iraq to invade Kuwait, believing that the Arab state system, embodied in the Arab League, with its prohibition against the invasion of one Arab state by another, would prevent the outbreak of war. Other governments believed that the troop movements were simply a show of force, intended to extract from Kuwait the maximum con-cessions possible.

When Iraq's surprise invasion of Kuwait took place on 2 August 1990, the attempts at mediation were to no avail – the Arab state system did not have the capacity to persuade Saddam Hussein back across the border. The international response was rapid and clear. The UN Security Council immediately passed a resolution declaring that the invasion was a breach of international peace and security. Successive UN resolutions led to economic sanctions against Iraq and a maritime blockade. Finally, it was declared that if Iraq had not withdrawn from Kuwait by 15 January 1991, a coalition of countries under the umbrella of the UN would be permitted to use armed force against it. This coalition united the USA and European states with Arab countries such as Egypt and Syria, positioned more than half a million non-Muslim troops in Saudi Arabia (an unprecedented development), and ensured that the invasion could not have a successful outcome.

This chain of events describes some of the circumstances leading to the invasion of Kuwait. It does not, however, explain them. Events are not in and of themselves the causes of other events. Events leading to war are made by people, by states and their intervention. Some states and leaders react to internal problems with external belligerence; others do not. Some border disputes are left almost permanently dormant or subdued; others are not. Some leaders are willing to gamble the destiny of their people in a war; others are not. The explanation of these variations and differences is an appropriate task for political theory.

This book attempts to disentangle the causes of the 1990 Gulf crisis using insights derived from political theory, and more specifically the theoretical framework set out in Kenneth Waltz's widely acclaimed *Man, the State and War*.[3] Waltz's framework – which will be examined in detail in the next chapter – is for several reasons particularly appropriate to such an enterprise. Firstly, the three categories it develops to throw light on the causes of conflict and war – man, the state and the international system – can be used as a basis for empirical as well as theoretical analysis. Secondly, in analysing a situation as complicated as the Gulf crisis, it has the advantage of proposing a complex approach to the problem of war: Waltz does not allow for simplistic single cause explanations which serve only to distort the true nature of war and the political framework in which it occurs. Thirdly, the use of a model of this kind offers the possibility of making generalised statements about the causes of wars in the modern Middle East without the cultural biases to which such explanations are usually subject. Thus this book firmly rejects one widespread Western point of view which suggests that somehow the Middle East is geopolitically and culturally unique and that wars which occur in that region are either an essential ingredient or an inevitable by-product of its culture.

Throughout the book the focus will be on the principal variables at play at key points leading up to and during the conflict. I will examine the historical, political, social and economic forces behind the Iraqi invasion of Kuwait and argue that the Gulf war resulted from a combination of elements: the leadership of Saddam Hussein, the nature of the Iraqi state, and the international system of states and that the crisis was precipitated by a peculiarly unstable combination of these elements. An alteration in even one of these factors would have brought forth a different set of political and diplomatic relationships and perhaps (although there is no certainty of this) a possibility for avoiding war.

Chapter 1

Theoretical Foundations:
Kenneth Waltz on War and Peace[1]

The pursuit of power through the waging of war has been an unfortunate constant of human interactions for millennia. The pattern of violence and suffering has long concerned scholars from all disciplines, and dominates much contemporary discussion of social and political behaviour. Conflict resolution and peace studies are enjoying renewed popularity, perhaps because of the end of the Cold War, but more likely because international conflict continues unabated.

A decision to go to war usually results from a complex set of variables. The Gulf crisis and war of 1990–91 was no exception. Waltz's analysis of the causes of war, based on what he calls the three 'images' of man, the state and the international system of states, will now be outlined. In the subsequent chapters this outline will form the basis for disentangling the particular set of political and economic complexities which led to the Gulf War. First, however, a word about Waltz's method of study is necessary.

Waltz's three fundamental images represent his own intellectual distillation of certain traceable patterns in political thinking on the causes of war. It is important to note that his theory is not comprehensive: it is not enough to notice the progression of images, starting with man, then moving on to the state, and ending with the international system of states. The essence of Waltz's approach lies not in his amalgamating three images or trends in thought, but in the particular way he balances these images in relationship to one another. The relationships between the images, as opposed to the images in and of themselves, is the theme which Waltz emphasises throughout his book.

He examines the writing of a number of political philosophers, concentrating mostly on St Augustine, Machiavelli, Spinoza, Kant and, at length, on Rousseau. He also examines types of thought, for example that of behavioural scientists, liberals and socialists. Throughout his book Waltz tries to find the relevance of past political thought to the problem of present-day war. His approach is to criticise the assumptions behind these various bodies of political thought, rather than to assess the value of their content. It is from Waltz's analysis of Rousseau that the pattern of the third image, the international system, emerges. Rousseau finds the major causes of war neither in man, nor in states, but in the state system itself. Waltz, however, takes this argument further and establishes his own approach to war by emphasising the relationship of the international system to the other two images, not by emphasising the international system as the most important image. For Waltz, the third image is the integrating factor which incorporates the other two images into the complex structure of causes that lead to war.

In Waltz's analysis, the prevention of war lies not in achieving perfection within any one single image, an impossible task in any case, but in negotiating the relationship between the three images in a way that promotes peace. The prevention of war lies not in the reform of mankind nor in the reform of states nor in the reform of the international system of states but in understanding the particular relationship between these three entities, and in understanding the paradoxical structure of conflicting political and economic needs which influence how that relationship develops to the point of breaking out in war.

Kenneth Waltz warns strongly against analysing the causes of war according to any one single image at the expense of the other two. Such analyses will inevitably be partial, limited and incomplete. The actions of states are influenced by their international environment; likewise, the international environment develops out of the nature of the states which it comprises. Man develops in relationship both to his state and to the international environment which limits his state, on the one hand, and encourages its growth, on the other. Finally, states are influenced by the nature of the men and women who govern and live within their national confines. Throughout the book the author describes a certain paradox involved when men, and the states they live in, operate to protect their own interests within a system of states: protecting a single man's or a single state's interest may destroy the very framework which allowed the single man or state to acquire interests in the first place. When war occurs, everybody loses, including the winners. Simple, single-cause explanations for Waltz clarify nothing.

It is the particular set of relationships which Waltz posits between men, the state and the international environment (the 'framework of action') which we will now attempt to outline.

Before presenting the argument, it is important to make one thing clear. Any summary of *Man, the State and War* is bound to represent a very simplified version of what is actually a complex argument. Throughout the book Waltz is dealing with certain core ideas on the one hand, and, on the other hand, interpreting the intellectual results of the different degrees of emphasis in the treatment of those ideas by political thinkers. In short, it is difficult to summarise his argument without stripping away his finely tuned and intricate structure of analysis. To an extent such simplification is inevitable. We hope, nevertheless, that we have here presented Waltz's work in a way which does his argument justice.[2]

The First Image: Man

Waltz begins his analysis of the causes of war with the problem of evil:

Is war simply mass malevolence, and thus an explanation of malevolence in explanation of the evils to which men in society are prey? Many have thought so ...

Our miseries are ineluctably the product of our natures. The root of all evil is man, and thus he is himself the root of the specific evil, war.[3]

This is the view of those thinkers who attribute the main cause of war to man's nature. It represents the basic theme of the political thinking which Waltz associates with first-image analysis on the causes of war. This view of war has been widespread and influential in political philosophy. St Augustine, Luther, Malthus, Jonathan Swift, Dean Inge, Reinhold Niebuhr and Spinoza have all inclined, to greater and lesser degrees, towards this view of war and its source in man's nature. In Waltz's words:

According to the first image of international relations, the locus of the important causes of war is found in the nature and behaviour of man. Wars result from selfishness, from misdirected impulses, from stupidity. Other causes are secondary and have to be interpreted in the light of these factors. If these are the primary causes of war, then the elimination of war must come through uplifting and enlightening men or securing their psychic-social re-adjustment. This estimate of causes and cures has been dominant in the writings of many serious students of human affairs from Confucius to present day pacifists. It is the leitmotif of many modern behavioural scientists as well.[4]

Waltz begins his argument, then, with the examination of the political and social prescriptions, which derive from this kind of first-image analysis and their intellectual limitations.

He starts with a core group of four writers: St Augustine, Spinoza, Hans Morgenthau and Reinhold Niebuhr. Although they have important differences, these writers share the view summarised by Waltz:

> Man is a finite being with infinite aspirations, a pygmy who thinks himself a giant. Out of his self-interest he develops economic and political theories and attempts to pass them off as universal systems; he is born and reared in insecurity and seeks to make himself absolutely secure; he is a man but thinks himself a god. The seat of evil is the self, and the quality of evil can be defined in terms of pride.[5]

These four thinkers share one basic intellectual tendency: to see political difficulties as the result of man's nature which has an inherent possibility for evil as well as for good. For Waltz, this is not necessarily an unreasonable position. There is no denying that politics derive from the political actions of men and that theories of politics must take into account man's nature. The problem which this position presents for political theory is that the definition of human nature, whatever it may be, is burdened with the impossible task of explaining an indefinite number of complex social and political events. How much actual difference human nature makes to the outcome of political actions is never possible to target with any precision. Moreover, if human nature is the cause of the outbreak of war it is also the reason wars end, and peace treaties are signed. Sometimes men go to war and sometimes they don't. That is as precise a conclusion that can be drawn from the premise that human nature is the main cause of war.

Clarifying this fundamental intellectual limitation of first-image thinking is Waltz's objective for the first part of his book.

Crucial to his analysis of first-image thinkers is the distinction which he draws between 'optimists' and 'pessimists'.[6] To put Waltz's distinction very simply: optimists believe in the possibility of progress and, through progress, in the imminent cessation of all war; pessimists believe that the final all-destructive military conflagration is just around the next corner. The simplicity of this definition should not obscure the true nature of the problem which it is meant to clarify. Few thinkers can readily be classified in one or the other category; there are varying degrees of optimism and pessimism in many theorists and in their systems of thought. According to Waltz:

> Pessimism in philosophy is the belief that reality is flawed, a thought expressed by Milton and Malthus ... Momentarily, more or less adequate restraints upon the forces of evil may be confined, but the expectation of a generally and permanently good result is presented by constant awareness of the vitiating effects of an essential defect. The optimist, on the other hand, believes that reality is good, society basically harmonious. The difficulties that have plagued men are superficial and momentary. The difficulties continue, for history is a succession of moments; but the quality of history can be changed, and the most optimistic believe that this can be done once and for all and rather easily. One comes back to expectations, but the expectations are rooted in different conceptions of the world.[7]

In distinguishing between optimists and pessimists, therefore, it must be remembered that the word pessimist does not necessarily indicate an attitude that completely despairs of a solution. Pessimists might well be very hopeful for a solution to war. What differentiates them from the optimists is the view of reality upon which their hopefulness is based. According to Waltz:

> The optimists see a possibility of turning the wicked into the good and ending the wars that result from present balance-of-power politics. The pessimists, while accepting the derivation of the balance of power and war from human natures see little if any possibility of man righting himself. Instead the balance of power is accorded an honourable position by them, for, it may truly keep people from tearing each other apart. And if occasionally it does not, still faulty prophylaxis is better than none at all.[8]

The influence of these different conceptions of the world on the political thinking of St Augustine, Spinoza, Niebuhr and Morgenthau is strong. All four writers indicate varying degrees of optimism and pessimism in their thinking, although Niebuhr and Morgenthau indicate the strongest tendency toward pessimism. They all draw political conclusions based upon an assumed nature of man. Spinoza's view of politics arises out of the notion that there is, in man, a conflict between reason and passion. On the other hand, St Augustine, Niebuhr and Morgenthau consider the whole man, mind and body, to be inherently defective. All of them, however, agree on a basic principle: political problems result from human defects. All of them are, therefore, limited in their understanding of what factors in human society generate political conflict.

To a certain extent this limitation has been recognised by the above-mentioned thinkers themselves. Spinoza explains political problems by relating them to the limitations of human nature, on the one hand, while, on the other hand he points out that under different conditions men behave differently.[9] There seems to be, in this case, a recognition that too much emphasis on one primary basic cause (i.e. human nature) serves to obscure the problem rather than clarify it.[10]

Secondary causes would seem also to be the more controllable causes and the areas more adequate for explaining differences. Niebuhr recognises the importance of balancing the emphasis of analysis when he says: 'The particular plight of modern civilisation is in a sense not caused by the sinfulness of human nature or by human greed. The greed of collective men must be taken for granted in the political order.'[11]

The main error of first-image analysis, which Niebuhr and Spinoza have recognised, has been its focus on human nature as a primary cause for war. Because human nature is complex, it can conceivably justify any number of hypotheses without actually clarifying anything.

The thinkers who, according to Waltz, focus on man as the most important cause of political arrangements and of war, do not necessarily all arrive at the same political remedy. Many of the thinkers who start with men as the locus of political action turn to the state or the state system, or some aspect of the two, when attempting to describe a prescription for avoiding war.

There is, however, a body of thought which remains within Waltz's first image of man for both the cause and remedy of war. These are the thinkers who argue that in order to end war, the nature of man must be somehow transformed. In assessing the underlying assumptions of this body of thought, Waltz presents the work of those modern behavioural scientists who have written on the subject of war and peace.

He begins with the claims of some modern social scientists that science applied to man in society can solve social problems, including war. The literature in this field has, according to Waltz, an obvious limitation: there is little evidence of any systematic attempt to relate the behavioural sciences to the problems of international politics. Very often the contribution of behavioural scientists to the problem of war has amounted to no more than saying that if men were all well-adjusted and rational the world would have peace. Their advice is effective, in other words, only if the problem is already solved.

The underlying assumption of the behavioural science approach is that the application of huge amounts of carefully researched data to social problems will bring about a transformation of society. Absent from the work of these behavioural scientists is any well developed theory of international politics. Remedies based on notions of human temperament and the process of upbringing and training have a very limited usefulness in relation to political problems. This failure to understand the connection between the political framework, and how man acts within that framework be it national or international, is what most limits the relevance of the behavioural sciences to political problems.

Waltz summarises the position of behavioural scientists as follows: 'The evilness of men, or their improper behaviour, leads to war; individual goodness, if it could be universalised would mean peace.'[12] There is in this way of thinking a naïveté about politics which works against their own efforts to solve political problems. That ineffectiveness derives from a view of man which is simplistic, and, therefore, useless. Both optimists and pessimists amongst the behavioural scientists of the first-image approach are at fault here. According to Waltz:

> To take either the position that men can be made good and then wars will cease to occur or the position that because men are bad wars and similar evils never will end may lead one to a consideration of social and political structure. If changing human nature will solve the problem, then one has to discover how to bring about the change ... The assumption of a fixed human nature in terms of which all else must be understood itself helps to shift attention *away* from human

nature – because human nature, by the terms of the assumption, cannot be changed, whereas social political institutions can be.[13]

This citation represents Waltz's second point of emphasis regarding first-image thinking. Human nature has something to do with the existence of war, but it also has something to do with the existence of just about everything from Sunday schools to brothels. Since human nature cannot possibly be the single determinant for the myriad of events which occur in politics, the need inevitably arises to consider other significant factors.

Many first-image thinkers take into account the role of the state but often in a way which subordinates its influence to that of human nature. In order to balance the view of war and its causes which these first-image thinkers convey, Waltz changes his focus, and, in the next section, considers the role of the state in the occurrence of war and the political thinking on war which emphasises the state.

The Second Image: The State

First-image thinking, focused on a defective human nature as the main cause of war, was best exemplified in Waltz's analysis by the work of behavioural scientists. Their attempt to explain politics and the problem of war entirely in terms of human psychology succeeded, eventually, in explaining nothing. It is not enough to understand human nature, even though there is no denying that human nature has something to do with the reason why wars break out. The problem of war cannot be understood without taking into account the influence which larger collectives, be they families, tribes, whole societies or states, have on the political actions that single human beings take. In Waltz's section on the state, he looks to the internal organisation of states as a means of understanding war, and why it occurs. In so doing he considers the following proposition: through the reform of states wars can be reduced or forever eliminated. Again, his primary concern is with the assumptions that thinkers make when they go from analysing causes to prescribing solutions. For this purpose Waltz focuses on the thought of nineteenth-century liberals, because of the principle underlying many of their arguments, that the internal dynamics of states determine their external behaviour.

The main thesis of late eighteenth- and nineteenth-century liberal thinking was that the internal conditions of states determined their external behaviour. Waltz begins his analysis of this thinking by considering their domestic political views. The dominant schools of thought during this period were individualistic and thereby reflected the influence of Hobbes (1588–1679). They did not share Hobbes's view of human nature (that man is basically egotistical and selfish and out to protect his own interests at all costs), nor did they accept his idea that selfish behaviour brought social benefits for the whole. Their view was that man was basically good and that, although individual behaviour had a selfish aspect, it also had within it enough natural social harmony to bring stability and progress to society.

According to liberal writers in nineteenth-century England (i.e. Adam Smith, John Stuart Mill, Jeremy Bentham), the state at its best ran smoothly because of the free play of individual initiative within the competition of the free market. The progress of mankind towards some future state of perfection was the source of progress for society. To restrain individuals and deny them freedom of action was harmful to society as a whole. Liberal thinking put a large amount of faith in mankind's moral and intellectual capacities and, therefore, did not contemplate a large role for government as a regulator of human affairs. They relied, instead, on the idea of the free-market regulator: the general interest of society, including production and the distribution of goods, would be superintended by the impersonal forces of the market.

At this point Waltz asks: is the assumption of nineteenth-century liberals and utilitarians, that society is self-regulatory, valid? He states an interesting paradox:

> Because a self-regulating society is a necessary means, in effect, it becomes part of the liberals' ideal end. If a laissez-faire policy is possible only on the basis of conditions described as necessary the laissez-faire ideal may itself require state action.[14]

In other words, laissez-faire works as an economic policy if the society in which it operates is designed to make it work. The idea that the system as a whole is entirely self-regulating does not stand up to scrutiny.

Liberal thinking accepts the necessity of the state, but seeks to circumscribe its role down to the absolute minimum. They exhibit a similar type of thinking when they turn from the nature and role of the state to international relations. When considering the notion of the state and the effect of its actions within the community of states, liberals accept the role of war, and then limit it.

Just as liberals and utilitarians assumed that society rested upon a foundation of harmonious interest, so, too, they assumed that the world community of states rested upon a foundation of constructive peaceful competition which would eventually advance the interests of all people. Royal families may seek to advance their interests through war but the real interests of all people in all societies are best enhanced by peace. If people were completely free to pursue their real interests national boundaries would cease to have any significance and people all over the world would engage in constructive competition.

In a world of free-trade laissez-faire states, war is not only foolish but economically useless. For a state to annex another state accomplishes nothing because the same advantages of such annexation can be had, at no cost to either state, by pursuing policies of free trade. The interests of the world's people are developed through increased production. The increase of production requires peace. The equitable distribution of that production requires that all people have the freedom to seek their interests anywhere in the world. This is the thinking behind the 'war does not pay' argument. It dates back at least to Emeric Crucé (early seventeenth century) and was later developed by Bentham and Mills. The point of this reasoning is to demonstrate the existence of an objective harmony of interests among states.

War does not pay. Peace is in everyone's real interests. These are eminently rational propositions. Why then, Waltz now asks, do states, nevertheless, pursue irrational political policies? If war does not pay why does it characterise relations between states?

The liberals would answer Waltz's question by saying that war gives greedy governments an excuse for raising taxes, expanding the bureaucracy and acquiring more control over its citizens. The stated political reasons for going to war are mere camouflages for the selfish motives of the statesmen who actually bring the wars about. The true interests of the people are ignored by governmental policy. If states were truly democratic, however, and the interests of the people were expressed in governmental policy, they would naturally tend towards peace. The people would control policy and their policy would favour peace.

In liberal political thinking, democracies are inherently peaceful. The basis of this idea was first developed by Kant who argued that war would be significantly reduced if the decision to go to war were left to the foot soldiers. Bentham also argued that the pressure of world public opinion could ensure a policy of peace if the statesmen of the world could be forced to recognise it.

This thinking represents a kind of complex utopianism. The liberals are not saying that all past wars would have been avoided if the people had been allowed to express their will. Crucial to their political thinking is the idea of progress. The liberal proposition is that the world and society have progressed to the point where war between states no longer need occur. History has brought mankind to the stage where reason can be made to prevail in both national and international affairs. States and individuals seek utility in their actions. Despotism, at this point in history (that is the late eighteenth and nineteenth centuries) will now fall away and democracy and the utility of the people will take its place.

Nineteenth-century liberal political thinking had some fundamental difficulties in practice, especially in its application to international relations and the prevention of war. The main practical problem derived from their assumptions. Their view of the state was based on the idea that human beings were infinitely perfectible, or, at least, able to improve themselves and that harmony or an inclination towards harmony guided man in his affairs within the state. Likewise their view of international relations was based on the idea that, given certain circumstances, states would proceed along the path of progress and achieve a state of harmony within themselves and with other states, so that war would become increasingly unlikely. Waltz asks, how, exactly, do states achieve this harmony amongst themselves? Furthermore, what is the point of adapting a laissez-faire approach to international relations when there is no way of ensuring that all states will practice it? If the non-interventionist logic of liberal thinking (represented by Kant, Cobden and Bright) is taken to its conclusion, then world peace is a matter of waiting for the political, social and economic forces of history to turn aggressive despotic states into peace loving democracies. Waltz questions whether the forces of history are moving fast enough and in the right direction, if at all.

The non-interventionist liberals would use force in international relations only where necessary to ensure democracy. A slightly different tendency in liberal thinking represented by Paine, Mazzini, and Wilson would pursue a policy to make the world democratic. There is a potential problem of hubris in this position. If peace is a good cause of war, the burden is upon peace-loving states to police the actions of despotic states. Wars become crusades for peace and democracy but they do not, thereby, decline in number, scale, or level of destruction. They are fought in the name of liberalism and tolerance but they kill the same number of people. Interventionist liberals start with a realistic position which rejects the assumption of automatic progress in history and which asserts that peace can only be brought about by actively eliminating the causes of war. The problem with this strand of liberal thinking is that it requires someone and something to be the moral judge in the affairs of states. Who is morally qualified to determine the justice, or its lack, exhibited by the actions of states is an impossible question to answer in any objective fashion.

Moreover, would the existence of a number of good peace-loving democratic states automatically lead to peace or, at least, a decrease in war? The liberal viewpoint did not necessarily anticipate a world in which there would be no political disputes. But if, as the liberals assumed, states are ever evolving and improving, then at some point war should decrease and states should develop the systematic means by which differences are settled rationally without armed force. But what, exactly, would such a system be? Would it be possible to devise such a system without ever requiring force to ensure its effectiveness? An international court of law or system of arbitration would not be a very effective entity without an organised force to back its decisions. Even within states, where courts of law are upheld in their effectiveness by the power of public opinion, there is still the need to back up the decisions of the court by force. Likewise, in the international arena, the power of international public opinion would not be enough to enforce the decisions of an international court.

Second-image analysis has the same problem as first-image analysis: it assumes the possibility of perfection in either man or in states. Since such perfection is impossible the liberal system can only ever provide an approximation of world peace and no guarantee that all states would willingly co-operate. In Waltz's words:

> ... the liberal prescription is impracticable, and the impracticability is directly related to the inadequacy of the liberal analysis. Peace with

justice requires an Organization with more and more of the qualities of government, just as informed justice was found to require an ever stronger and more active government.[15]

In short, the analysis of international relations according to the second image is inadequate.

The statement that bad states lead to war has a large amount of truth in it. The obverse statement, that good states bring peace to the world, is not necessarily true and is, in fact, extremely doubtful. To say that men make the societies and the international environment in which they live is true, but only to a certain extent. The whole truth is that the societies and the international community in which they live also make men. Furthermore, the actions of states and of men acting within states are the structure of international relations.

The Third Image:
International Conflict and International Anarchy

Third-image thinking derives from the idea that the many sovereign states of the world coexist in a condition of anarchy. There is no system of enforceable law to control the actions of these states. Each state determines its acts of aggression or its resistance to aggression according to its own political criteria. In such a state of international anarchy conflict is bound to occur and war seems to be inevitable. Each state is completely dependent on its own devices. Each state is, therefore, constantly concerned with its capacity to cope with the possible aggression of other states. Third-image thinking differentiates itself from second-image thinking through this emphasis on international anarchy. The idea of states achieving harmony amongst themselves, prevalent in second-image thinking, does not have much currency here. In Waltz's words:

> In anarchy there is no automatic harmony ... A state will use force to attain its goals if, after assessing the prospects for success, it values those goals more than it values the pleasures of peace. Because each state is the final judge of its own cause, any state may at any time use force to implement its policies. Because any state may at any time use force, all states must constantly be ready either to counter force with force or to pay the cost of weakness. The requirements of state action

are in this view, imposed by the circumstances in which all states exist.[16]

Waltz's main point, that the causes of war are best understood by balancing the three intellectual images or patterns which he traces in his book and by allowing scope for the interdependence of these three images upon each other, comes into clear focus with his discussion of the third image. According to Waltz:

> In a manner of speaking, all three images are a part of nature. So fundamental are man, the state and the state system in any attempt to understand international relations that seldom does an analyst, however wedded to one image, entirely overlook the other two. Still, emphasis on one image may distort one's interpretation of the others.[17]

In his analyses of first- and second-image thinking, Waltz indicated that a certain amount of naïveté and ungrounded optimism often results from emphasising one image at the expense of others. That is because focusing on one image alone allows the observer to ignore the inherent difficulties of the problem, difficulties which would become very apparent if the situation was viewed from a different angle. The result, as we have seen, is that the prescriptions for avoiding or limiting war which derive from this thinking add up to little more than utopianism. The same limitation is manifested in third-image thinking. The difference here, however, is that it offers the possibility of integrating the points of view of the first and second images and can thereby lead to a realistic understanding of the complex factors which cause war and how those factors might be controlled or at least mitigated.

The focus of Waltz's analysis of third-image thinking is on the political thought of Rousseau. In his theory of international relations, Rousseau is primarily concerned with the international and political environment and the qualities of states. Rousseau maintains that the existence of a number of good states would not necessarily produce a peaceful world. What is right and just for the internal politics of any particular state does not necessarily constitute an equitable political agenda for the rest of the world. The best governed state can, even with the best intentions, enter upon an unjust war. In order to achieve world peace, particular separate states have to subordinate their separate wills to the community of states. As long as there is no authority above the community of states to adjudicate in cases of political conflict, war will be inevitable. Waltz summarises the main point of Rousseau's theory of international relations: 'That among particularities accidents will occur is not accidental but necessary. And this in turn is simply another way of saying that in anarchy there is no automatic harmony.'[18] Any individual state can be rational and predictable from its own political point of view, and arbitrary and ruthless from the point of view of other states.[19] A perfectly good state, in other words, can easily provoke the violent resistance of other states. Rousseau's theory is clearly based on the European system of states, which according to him must inevitably clash. Not a single one of them can move without upsetting another. Why? Because in the words of Rousseau, their union is 'formed and maintained by nothing better than chance.'[20]

Or as Waltz's summarises it: 'The nations of Europe are wilful units in close juxtaposition with rules neither clear nor enforceable to guide them.'[21]

The community of European states does not represent, for Rousseau, a situation in which it is realistic to expect some kind of automatic harmony of interest and automatic agreement on matters of rights and duties. What lies behind this lack of harmony? Is it caused by the states who act according to their own self-interest or by the system of states within which they act? Rousseau's answer emphasises the system rather than the separate states. However, he does not necessarily discount the effect of the acts of separate states. In Waltz's words:

> It is the specific acts that are the immediate causes of war, the general structure that permits them to exist and wreak their disasters. To eliminate every vestige of selfishness, perversity and stupidity in nations would serve to establish perpetual peace, but to try directly to eliminate all the immediate causes of war without altering the structure of the 'Union of Europe' is utopian.[22]

Rousseau rejects the idea of Kant, that a voluntary federation could keep peace among the European states. In Rousseau's words, the remedy for war,

> ... is to be found only in such a form of federal government as shall unite nations by bands similar to those which already unite their individual members, and place the one no less than the other under the authority of law.[23]

Rousseau's solution raises obvious questions. Could this federation enforce its law on the member-states without recourse to war? Rousseau argued that the political balance between the states of Europe was so finely tuned that no one state or combination of states could ever establish a hegemony over the others.

However impractical Rousseau's proposed solution might be, his theoretical analysis of war as the result of international anarchy cannot be entirely disregarded. There is some truth to his assertion that war occurs because there is nothing to prevent it. Both war and peace derive as much from the 'framework of action' as from actions themselves.

Closely associated with Rousseau's third-image analysis is the concept of 'balance of power'. No one state has complete freedom of action. The actions of one state are limited by the actions of the others. A certain balance of power also exists within states, but it is of a different order. While the use of force is usually controlled by the state in domestic politics, there is no authority in international politics capable of exercising the same type of monopoly. To speak of a balance of power among states is to speak of a balance of the capacities of those states, especially their capacities to use force against each other.

Although some political thinkers have denied the existence of any real balance of power amongst the world's states,[24] Waltz asserts that it is not an illusion and that politicians who pretend to be above balance of power politics do so at their peril. Especially in foreign policy it is difficult if not impossible for any state to maintain its security without recognising the maxim: 'Everybody's strategy depends on everybody else's.'

A good illustration of this balance of power maxim comes from the game theory of John von Neumann and Oskar Morgenthau. In order to win a game involving two or more players, even a simple card game, a player needs to devise a strategy which takes into account the strategies of the other players. In a situation where there are three or more players, the possibility will arise for some of those players to form a coalition against another player. Such a case might arise when one particular player or group of players is in a position to win the game quickly, unless he is stopped by concerted opposition. The opposition will unite to confront a common enemy, even though they might have been at enmity amongst themselves very recently.

On the other hand, no coalition may be formed at all. The element of dislike or of sheer stupidity amongst the players may be such that co-operating, even for mutual advantage, isn't possible. In addition the situation might be one in which it becomes very difficult or impossible to judge the right moment for forming a coalition. When the idea of coalition is rejected under these circumstances, the players involved have either missed the point of the game or have decided, for whatever reasons, either that the game cannot be won or is not worth winning.

In order to understand the applicability of game theory to the actions of states in international politics, a certain amount of elaboration on the game theory is required. A card game, like poker, is a zero-sum game: what one player wins, another player loses. The game begins with a certain amount of money on the table. At the end of the game the same amount of money remains on the table, but in the hands of a different player. The problem is one of distribution, not of new production.

The political activities of men and states do not always correspond to this zero-sum model because the problem may be one of production as well as of distribution. What one group gains is not necessarily equal to other groups' losses. In fact, the strategies of the various groups may coalesce in such a way that advantages accrue to all the groups involved. There might result a general increase in productivity in which all can partake because of the particular way in which each group changes strategy in response to another group's changed strategy. One of two things can happen in this case. Either all the groups bond together in order to increase production to the fullest extent possible; or the groups involved become so concerned with dividing the goods already in existence that they forget about any further co-operation to produce more goods. The latter possibility is often what happens in international politics: the gain of one group or coalition is often considered to be the loss of the other. This was usually the perception underlying relations between America and the Soviet Union during the Cold War.

States have a certain amount of choice among these alternatives but one factor remains constant: the will to survive. Some states might want to conquer the whole world, some states might want to conquer only a part of it, and some states might just want to be left alone. Even the state that wants to conquer the world has also to think about continuing its existence. On the other hand, even the state that wants to be left alone is never free and clear of having to consider the strategies of other states. Waltz summarises this:

The implication of game theory, which is also the implication of the third image, is that the freedom of choice of any one state is limited by the actions of all others. And this limitation applies as much to the process of deciding which game to play as it does to the actual playing of the game.

Given a sufficient number of players engaged in a competitive game, von Neumann and Morgenthau demonstrate with convincing mathematical rigor the possible advantages of combinations among them. The clever player will be on the watch for a chance to increase his gains or cut his losses by co-operating with another. Similarly in international politics, so long as the participants do not consider themselves players of a game in which all concentrate on production and none worries about distribution, states will ever be tempted to form coalitions for the simple reason that those who combine acquire an advantage over those who do not. If some states seek an advantage over others, they combine. If the advantage sought is measured in terms of power to destroy or damage another state then the threatened state refrains from the effort to increase its strength only at the risk of its survival. Pursuing a balance-of-power policy is still a matter of choice, but the alternatives are those of probable suicide on the one hand and the active playing of the power-politics game on the other. The factors that distinguish international politics from other games are: (1) that the stakes of the game are considered to be of unusual importance and (2) that in international politics the use of force is not excluded as a means of influencing the outcome. The cardinal rule of the game is often taken to be: Do whatever you must in order to win it. If some states act on this rule or are expected to act on it, other states must adjust their strategies accordingly.[25]

There is an important difference between balance of power politics on the international level and balance of power politics within states. In domestic politics the state, for the most part, has a monopoly on the use of physical force. In international politics such a monopoly does not exist. There is no one authority with effective control over the use of force by the world's many states. The balance of power among states is in fact the balance of their capacities to use force in dealing with other states.

The balance of power game[26] in international politics is not inevitable. Its existence will continue, however, as long as states need to defend their survival in a condition of anarchy among states. As Waltz concludes:

In summary, then, it can be said that the balance of power is not so much imposed by statesman on events as it is imposed by events on statesman. It is not to be eliminated by declaration but, if it is to be eliminated at all, by altering the circumstances that produce it. The circumstances are simply the existence of a number of independent states that wish to remain independent. Freedom is implied in the word 'independence' but so is the necessity of self-reliance. Competition takes a number of forms, but the units in all systems of competition tend to drive for favoured positions. If the drive of some units appears to promise success, it is blocked by other units whose similar motives cause them in turn to counter and thrust. Where an effective law-enforcing authority exists, balance is measured in terms other than force. Where there is nothing to prevent the use of force as a means of altering the terms and the results of competition, the capacity to use force tends to become the index by which the balance of power is measured. No system of balance functions automatically. A drive for hegemony by any one state may be successful despite the resistance of other states, or for some reason the other states may not resist; but under certain conditions, conditions that have often existed in international politics, systems of balance do develop. If a condition of balance becomes the conscious goal of states, then one would expect the balancing process to be one of greater precision and subtlety. In the midst of a large number of roughly equal states, competition is intense and the balancing process intricate.[27]

Waltz discusses some significant historical examples which invite the interpretation of third-image thinking. During the eighteenth and nineteenth centuries there came to fruition the European balance of power systems in which states shifted their allegiance from one coalition to another in a game of chessboard diplomacy. With the end of the nineteenth century, and especially with the outbreak of the First World War, the scale of these political shifts has changed, but a balance of power amongst the states of the West (as there is amongst the states of the world)[28] continues, nevertheless, to be a pattern. Changes in technology and economics have induced political changes which make the model of nineteenth-century balance of power politics no longer entirely applicable, but fundamental points still exist on which there is continuity.

From 1890, the alliance system which had been inaugurated by Bismarck in 1879, was on its way to becoming a two bloc system. Under such circumstances mobilisation was all but inevitable. Once mobilisation began it became general and that meant war. The situation in Europe before the First World War offers a strong confirmation of third-image thinking, since it is a prime example of everybody's strategy depending upon everybody else's. Waltz's explanation, however, offers a good example of how first- and second-image thinking can be integrated with the third.

The objection is valid, that the third image alone cannot possibly explain why any country should want to mobilise in the first place and therefore it cannot explain the outbreak of the First World War.

Austria and Germany feared Russia because of its growing economy and population and because the Tsar was not in easy control of his throne and was therefore unlikely always to follow a policy of moderation. France feared Germany because of its growing economy and strong military. England shared the same fear of Germany and of her ability to overturn the balance of Europe upon which British security traditionally rested. In the words of Waltz:

> The alliance system was proclaimed by some to be a system of security. It was. Each step in its formation, from the Dual Alliance to the British–Russian Entente, has to be explained largely in terms of the attempts of the participants to get out from under a feeling of danger to themselves. The states of Europe combined and recombined, Italy being the greatest recombiner, until they stood face to face with lines drawing tighter in each moment of crisis.
>
> This was a security system – but only until someone jiggled. The game of European power politics had become with rough equivalence a two-person, zero-sum game. A gain for any one state became a gain for its side and simultaneously a loss for the other. A single move then had a double effect, and, with the two sides roughly balanced, neither could permit the other the gain that would be its own loss as well. Believing that mobilisation meant war may have helped to make it so, but there were other factors as well, among them the closeness of the balance that made the area of manoeuvre narrower than is sometimes thought. In June 1914, the seemingly small matter of Serbia involved not only the prestige but also the security of both sides. Because Russia could not afford to let Austria have her own way with Serbia she reacted; because Germany could not afford to let Austria back down, she reacted; and so on around the vicious and tragic circle. Some would call it a meaningless circle as well.[29]

The same difficulties in European balance of power politics lay behind the start of the Second World War. In the late 1930s Neville Chamberlain tried to apply the lesson of the First World War and sought to avoid giving Germany cause for alarm. He failed to understand the nature of the political relationships which he confronted. Appeasement can sometimes serve only to weaken the position of the appeaser, especially if the favoured state has extremely ambitious political goals.

A peaceful, appeasing state has a way of encouraging a war of aggression from another state. This is the lesson to be learned from the First and Second World Wars.

> ... a balance of power may result either because most states seek it or because some states react to the drive for preponderance of others. Where a balance of power does exist, it behoves the state that desires peace as well as safety to become neither too strong nor too weak ... the seeming aggressiveness of one state may invite a war of prevention that a more pacific pose might have avoided altogether. There is in international politics no simple rule to prescribe just how belligerent, or how peaceful, any given state should strive to appear in order to maximise its chances of living at peace with neighbouring states. One cannot say in the abstract that for peace a country must arm, or disarm, or compromise, or stand firm. One can only say that the possible effects of all such policies must be considered.
>
> The third image makes this clear. The peace strategy of any one country must depend on the peace or war strategies of all other countries. As competition in international politics becomes more intense, a process that none of the arch competitors acting alone can prevent, the peace-loving state faces the necessity of balancing between too little and too much strength, between too many failures that strengthen the potential enemy and too many successes that scare him unduly.[30]

Conclusion

Waltz's purpose in *Man, the State and War* is not to provide a model of world peace for government policy makers but to examine the assumptions upon which models and political thinking on war and peace (the 'images' of Waltz's argument) are based. Politicians and political thinkers are as influenced by their own private assumptions as they are by the world's events.

The images in political thinking which Waltz categorises into three main trends have gone in and out of vogue at various times over the last two centuries. The logic of many balance of power approaches to international relations, that peaceful states existing within an order of international anarchy sometimes have to consider undertaking a preventative war, is manifest in the writings of Thucydides, Alexander Hamilton, Machiavelli, Hobbes and Rousseau. Their main idea is that the nature of any one particular state is significantly determined by the nature of its relationship to other states.

Leopold Ranke (1795–1886) applied this idea to the history of the states of modern Europe. He argued that the external relations of states determine their internal conditions. During the nineteenth century, such an argument made sense. Diplomacy amongst European statesmen was all important; the influence of the techniques of diplomacy on the thinking of statesmen was pervasive. How statesmen conducted the internal affairs of their states was usually a reflection of how they conducted affairs with other states. But even by the beginning of the nineteenth century there had emerged a tendency to think in terms of the factors internal to states as the more important influence in international relations, and to explain relations among states in terms of their internal condition.

Waltz demonstrates throughout his book that the vogue of an image varies with time and place. Although no single image has ever been emphasised in political thinking at the expense of the other two, the degree to which one particular image gains prominence in a trend of thought strongly influences how the other two images are interpreted and incorporated. The predominant point of Waltz's argument is, in fact, that focusing mainly on one image in analysing the causes of war distorts the other two. This aspect of Waltz has already been made sufficiently clear. We will conclude by looking at the particular effects which result from focusing primarily on the third image.

The third image is very similar to the first and second images in that it results in utopian prescriptions for avoiding war. In third-image thinking, the possibility of war will always be among us as long as two or more states exist and protect their own interest within a world order devoid of any higher agency to which they might appeal for protection or some kind of arbitration. As in the case of the other two images, one cause is identified and everything else is interpreted in terms of that cause. One type of third-image thinking argues, therefore, for a system of world government without offering any realistic assessment of the ease with which it might be realised nor of its probable effectiveness as a counter to civil wars or even world wars. The result is the same as it is with first- and second-image thinking: an airtight tautology (good men or good states will not be violent; an effective international organisation will not allow violence) based on statements which are possibly true but somehow make no real difference to the actual course of world politics. In the words of Waltz:

> The belief that to make the world better requires changing the factors that operate within a precisely defined realm leads to despair whenever it becomes apparent that changes there, if possible at all, will come slowly and with insufficient force.[31]

Arguing instead for an approach which integrates all three images to arrive at an analysis engaging the political problem of war in its full complexity, Waltz continues:

> The contrary assertion, that all causes may be interrelated, is an argument against assuming that there is a single cause that can be isolated by analysis and eliminated or controlled by wisely constructed policy. It is also an argument against working with one or several hypotheses without bearing in mind the interrelation of all causes. The prescriptions directly derived from a single image are incomplete because they are based upon partial analyses. The partial quality of each image sets up a tension that drives one toward inclusion of the others. With the first image the direction of change representing Locke's perspective as against Plato's, is from men to societies and states. The second image catches up both elements. Men make states and states make men, but this is still a limited view. One is led to a search for the more inclusive nexus of causes, for states are shaped by the international environment as are men by both the national and international environments.[32]

Waltz's conclusion is to suggest an intellectual structure in which the three images can be interrelated without distorting any one of them.

The third image is his starting point because its emphasis on the framework of action, especially in the writings of Rousseau, clarifies the misleading aspects of partial analyses and the unrealistic expectations which they inspire. If the third image is not interpreted as a theory of world government but as a theory of the conditioning effects of the state system, it makes clear that, as far as promoting peace is concerned, no single act is good in and of itself. What makes an act good or moral in an individual might make the same act an incitement to violence if performed by a state. The policy of appeasement adopted by England in the 1930s did not prevent the First World War and possibly did much to make it unavoidable.

Rousseau's analysis, in which war is considered to be the consequence of the framework of state action, represents according to Waltz a significant step forward towards finding the 'nexus of causes' that lead to war. That is because Rousseau's explanation does not depend on what Waltz would call 'accidental causes' (p. 231) such as defects in men or states. His theory is, rather, that the framework of action is such that any accident can bring about a war. In other words, wars occur because there is nothing to prevent them.

In Rousseau's analysis, the effect of the state system is not direct. If state A attacks state B, the more direct causes would probably be found in a first- or second-image analysis. The actions of both states might be influenced by location, size, power, interest, type of government, past history and tradition. The policy makers of each state would have their own particular explanation for the outbreak of war based on a combination of these specific immediate factors. A change in any one or even in all of those specific factors, however, would not necessarily prevent war. That is because the international environment within which these factors operate constitutes a crucial part of what causes war. In the words of Waltz:

> Two points are omitted from the prescriptions we considered under the first and second images: (1) If an effect is produced by two or more causes, the effect is not permanently eliminated by removing one of them. If wars occur because men are less than perfectly rational and because states are less than perfectly formed, to improve only states may do little to decrease the number and intensity of wars. The error here is in identifying one cause where two or more may operate. (2) An endeavour launched against one cause to the neglect of others may make the situation worse instead of better. Thus, as the Western democracies became more inclined to peace Hitler became

more belligerent. The increased propensity to peace of some participants in international politics may increase rather than decrease the
likelihood of war. This illustrates the role of the permissive cause, the
international environment. If there were but two loci of cause involved, men and states, we could be sure that the appearance of more
peacefully inclined states would, at worst, not damage the cause of
world peace. Whether or not a remedy proposed is truly a remedy or
actually worse than none at all depends, however, on the content and
timing of the acts of all states. This is made clear in the third image.[33]

Waltz is arguing for an interrelation of efficient (first and second
images) and permissive (third image) causes. A conflict can arise from
disputes born of specific issues, which, in retrospect, appear to be trivial.
To focus on these immediate issues as the main cause of any war,
however, leads nowhere. Such causes never provide sufficient explanation for the wars that have occurred. To argue, for instance, that mutual
fear of modern weapons amongst states might give those states sufficient
cause for avoiding war, indicates a dangerous over-simplification of why
states go to war. The same fear might, under a different set of circumstances, induce several states to go to war. No solution to the problem
of war is possible by concentrating solely on one of the three images.

Instead, the solution, according to Waltz, is to view the first and
second images in the perspective of the third.[34] The third image
provides the theoretical basis for Waltz's conclusion that:

> ... in the absence of tremendous changes in the factors included in
> the first and second images, war will be perpetually associated with
> the existence of separate sovereign states.[35]

Third-image analysis can lead to the utopian conclusion that world
government is the remedy for world war; a remedy which is not possible
on a practical level. On the other hand, it can be the basis for a realistic
approach to the problem of war:

> If everyone's strategy depends upon everyone else's, then the Hitlers
> determine in part the action, or better, reaction of those whose ends
> are worthy and whose means are fastidious. No matter how good their
> intentions, policy makers must bear in mind the implications of the
> third image, which can be stated in summary form as follows: Each
> state pursues its own interests, however defined, in ways it judges best.
> Force is a means of achieving the external ends of states because

there exists no consistent, reliable process of reconciling the conflicts of interest that inevitably arise among similar units in a condition of anarchy. A foreign policy based on this image of international relations is neither moral nor immoral but embodies merely a reasoned response to the world about us. The third image describes the framework of world politics, but without the first and second images there can be no knowledge of the forces that determine policy; the first and second images describe the forces in world politics, but without the third image, it is impossible to assess their importance or predict their results.[36]

The question remains: How can Waltz's analysis, which is exclusively based on Western politics and diplomatic history be useful for understanding the causes of the Gulf War? We have already seen that Waltz is not prescribing a model by which to analyse war. Rather, he is criticising the assumptions behind such models which have been prescribed by other thinkers. If we look at the relationships which Waltz posits between first-, second- and third-image thinking, however, much of his approach to the analysis of war can be applied to understanding events in the Middle East.

In applying to Middle Eastern affairs the idea of the international system of states which is fundamentally derived from the system of states which developed in Europe, it must be emphasised that today's Middle Eastern states were created in a somewhat arbitrary fashion after the First World War and the fall of the Ottoman empire. The political, religious, ethnic and cultural fabric of the Middle East is such that it divides up into nation states with far less ease and inherent geographical logic than Europe. The Ottoman empire, despite its many failings, had been a unifying and therefore valuable political force. The state system of the modern Middle East is inherently unstable because it was imposed from the outside by the political agenda of European statesmen. Under the highly fraught circumstances of the late nineteenth and early twentieth centuries the Middle East did not have the time to develop its own internal political solution to the fall of the Ottoman empire. Since that time, the region has been beset by two conflicting tendencies: a drive towards political, religious and ethnic factionalism on the one hand, and a search to find a basis for political unity and integrity on the other. Both tendencies are, in a way, results of the Ottoman legacy.

The Middle East, therefore, both attracts and resists the political ambitions of hegemonist leaders, the type of which Saddam Hussein is a very good example. We will see in the subsequent chapters how Saddam Hussein's bid for hegemony in the region combined with an inherently unstable political structure within the Middle East and a changed, untested, post-Cold War political climate in the international arena to bring on the Gulf War. Our analysis of Kenneth Waltz will allow us to put all these factors into a useful perspective.

Chapter 2

Saddam Hussein

The main point of Waltz's book, *Man, the State and War*, is that no useful analysis of the causes of war can be done by focusing exclusively on one image. Saddam Hussein's leadership was not the sole cause nor the determining cause of the Gulf war. That does not mean, however, that he had nothing to do with the causes of the Gulf war. His dominance of Iraqi politics and his style of leadership is such that an overview of the factors that shaped his character is in order. The force of Saddam Hussein's leadership created an unstable relationship between Iraq and other Middle Eastern states, on the one hand, and Iraq and the major Western powers on the other. This is not to say that he created the Gulf war by himself but that he was a key factor in bringing the crisis to a head and that he had a considerable impact on a set of political relationships which were already unstable.

Saddam Hussein has been at the centre of politics in Iraq for a quarter of a century. For eleven years, he was the country's second highest official, and for more than twelve has been its undisputed leader. Two years after assuming the presidency, he entered his first foreign adventure, a war with Iran which lasted for eight years. Two years later he plunged his country into another external conflict, the invasion of Kuwait, ever since which Iraq has been under an unrelenting international siege. Since Saddam Hussein assumed the presidency, Iraq has enjoyed only two years of peace. His rule has also produced Iraq's longest stretch of political stability since the days of colonialism. How Saddam Hussein has succeeded in maintaining his extraordinary position will be a major theme of this chapter.

The death of President Gamal Abdel Nasser of Egypt in 1971 marked the beginning of a new era in contemporary Arab politics. The generation of Arab leaders who were the founding fathers of Arab nationalism was essentially idealistic, and dedicated to the creation of a single Arab nation.[1] But, as it became clear that this high ambition had failed, a new brand of Arab leader came to power, exemplified by men like Hafez al-Assad in Syria and Saddam Hussein in Iraq. While they still paid lip service to party slogans, these leaders abandoned any serious pretence of an ideological crusade and moved to the 'right', becoming closet realists as they realised how much their countries (and they themselves) might gain from pursuing their own narrow political and national interests. Majid Khadduri, among others, has pointedly noted that 'the pendulum has swung almost completely from the ideological to the realist position ... The leaders who dominate the political scene today belong essentially to the realist school.'[2]

Although both the pessimistic and the optimistic, the realistic and the idealistic views of man need to be taken into account in any examination of Iraq's leader, the violence of Saddam Hussein's actions suggests that the pessimistic, or realistic view, which develops from an acceptance of man's violent nature, will help to explain his decisions on war and peace. This chapter will examine the formative influences in Saddam Hussein's childhood, and his domestic and parental circumstances, and assess their influence on his adult political attitudes and his complex psychological make-up. The perseverance Saddam needed for his ascent to power in Iraq and the skilful political manoeuvring he employed to assure his political survival will also be analysed, and their political effects evaluated.

The chapter will also evaluate the leadership of Saddam Hussein, and examine his distinctive contribution to the 1990 invasion of Kuwait and the 1980 invasion of Iran. It is clear that Iraq without Saddam at the helm would have been a far more peaceful and predictable nation, which would probably not have embarked upon the military adventures which are now an inescapable and gloomy fact of Iraqi history.

Saddam Hussein's Childhood

Saddam Hussein was born on 28 April 1937 in al-Auja, near Takrit. The name Saddam comes from an Arabic word whose meaning is literally 'to punch' or 'to strike'. It has thus been translated in several officially-approved biographies, with some justification, as 'the fighter who stands steadfast'.[3] Interestingly, in such biographies, details of his childhood and upbringing are not at all clear. It can be inferred that Saddam Hussein prefers to keep the harshness and brutality of his childhood to himself. He has instead attempted to foster a new persona, a myth that supports his own image of himself as a man, sprung from nowhere, whose spontaneous and superhuman qualities have made him a great leader and prospective saviour of the Arab nation.[4]

A number of outside observers, on the other hand, see Saddam as a man driven by an inferiority complex created by the trauma of his childhood experiences, the bitterness of which has haunted him ever since. Saddam Hussein had a fatherless childhood; some reports claim that his father died before his son was born, while others allege that the father simply abandoned his wife and child. In either case, Saddam's sense of rejection cannot have been lessened when his mother re-married. Her new husband was the already-married Ibrahim al-Hassan, a crude, brutal and illiterate peasant who resented Saddam and abused him both physically and psychologically. For example, to show his contempt for the boy, al-Hassan reportedly used to send his own son to school while demanding that Saddam work in the fields.[5] In addition, contrary to Arab custom, the young Saddam was raised in the house, a humble mud-brick affair, that his mother shared with her new husband. Because of the step-father's reputation (he was known locally as 'Hassan the Liar') and the unusual situation at home, the boy is said by Bulloch and Morris to have been considered an outcast by other children.[6] He got into fights rather frequently, and when neighbours complained about him, al-Hassan's response was to blame Saddam's mother. 'He is the son of a cur,' he would tell her. 'Send him away.'

Saddam Hussein did not actually begin his education until he was ten years old. At that time his relationship with his stepfather had deteriorated still further and the young boy was either kicked out of the house or simply ran away. His relations with some members of his extended family were better, and he chose to move in with his uncle Khairallah, whose deep hatred for imperialism and admiration for the Nazis influenced Saddam from his early days.[7] Life with his uncle was less than ideal in other ways: Khairallah often sent the boy to steal for him from the villagers, a habit that eventually landed Saddam, if only briefly, in a juvenile detention centre.

Life in the village of Takrit in Iraq was similar to that in many neighbouring countries. Not only were the basic necessities of life lacking, but health conditions at the time were appalling. In 1937, for example, the year Saddam was born, one in every three babies born in any Iraqi village was destined to die. From these terribly harsh personal, social, and economic circumstances, Saddam surely learned some hard lessons about the survival of the fittest early in the formative years of his life.[8]

Such was the reality of Saddam's childhood and adolescence: fatherless, he was lonely, friendless, and ridiculed by his village contemporaries to such an extent that he used to walk around the village with an iron rod to protect himself. Some of his political opponents claim that he would heat this rod in a fire until it turned red-hot, and then jab at a passing animal with it.[9]

At the age of ten, according to two official biographies possibly concerned with promoting the image of a fearless fighter, Saddam was already familiar with the use of fire-arms. According to Karsh and Rautsi, at the age of 21 he was implicated in the killing of a civil servant, for which he was arrested and later released for lack of evidence.[10]

By the time he had moved to Baghdad in his late teens, he was powerfully built and physically imposing and, it has been claimed, had already established 'a reputation as a murderer and a thug'. He was what his environment had made him, having grown up in what Bulloch and Morris describe as an atmosphere 'of corruption, lawlessness and murder. The family were of lowly peasant background, but were feared as local brigands. This was a community in which casual violence and even murder enhanced the reputation of the perpetrator.'[11]

Political Formation

Saddam clearly possessed qualities which facilitated his rapid climb to the highest office in one of the most volatile states in the Middle East. As one admirer observed, these qualities included 'patience, prudence, and courage, combined with ambition and single-mindedness'.[12]

The most formative years for the development of Saddam's political character were the 1930s and 1940s. Mirroring the upheavals of the war in Europe, Arab national sentiment was expressed in passionate intellectual debate. As in other idealistic, struggling nations remote from the harsh realities of the European war, admiration for Mussolini and

Hitler was running high in some quarters of Iraq. Despite the country's
independence, Britain still enjoyed preferential treatment due to a
bilateral treaty negotiated with the Iraqi royal family, which allowed
Britain two military bases on Iraq's territory. Militant nationalists as a
result supported Nazi Germany and looked forward to a Nazi victory,
which could weaken Britain and dislodge her from the entire Middle
East.[13] There were also those who leaned toward a popular socialism
modelled on that of the British Labour Party. Even so, despite the
existence of diverse groups of anti-Fascist, even Marxist intellectuals,
all were united in their antipathy toward Britain as a colonial power.[14]
This feeling was reinforced by a deep resentment of Britain's continuing
influence in the Middle East and its considerable military presence in
Iraq.

    This situation had a profound effect on Saddam's political attitudes.
His uncle, who was then an officer in the army, was jailed for particip-
ating in an unsuccessful coup attempt against the monarchy; his military
career was ruined as a result of his participation in the plot. Thereafter
he harboured a deep resentment of the monarchy and of the foreign
powers supporting it, and he passed his ardour on to his impressionable
young nephew. According to Saddam Hussein himself, the greatest
influence shaping his political views at that early age were the memoirs
of the leader of the failed coup.[15] His official biography claims that
when the twenty-year-old joined the passionately nationalistic Ba'th
party in 1957, it was principally because of the ideals of nationalism
instilled in him when his mother recounted the stories of his uncle's
valiant fight against the British during the revolution in 1941. The
nationalist opposition to the British had resulted in the death of some
of his relatives and the burning of their houses.[16] The nature and power
of these events increased the influence of Saddam's uncle on his
nephew. His uncle Khairallah 'played the role of father to the boy and
was his object of male identification. As both model and mentor, he
nurtured the nationalistic sentiments of the young Saddam. He intro-
duced Saddam to people who were to play a key role in his rise to
power, including the future president, Ahmed Hassan al-Bakr,
Khairallah's cousin and close friend throughout the 1940s and 1950s.'[17]

    According to his official biographies, Saddam Hussein waged a
remarkable and ceaseless campaign of self-improvement, despite
tremendous difficulties and challenges. Even the very first years of his

schooling were achieved in the face of his family's objections and despite a long distance between his home and the school.[18] Later, the boy studied at the excellent Kharkh school, and went on at the age of eighteen to an important secondary school in Baghdad.[19] Nevertheless, sophisticated Iraqis still detect an accent and grammatical errors in Saddam's speech patterns which betray his origins.[20]

At the age of ten, when Saddam first went to school, he reportedly did not know how to spell his name, and diverted attention from himself by making fun of his teacher instead, amusing his classmates by putting a snake up under the teacher's robe.[21] It may have been his uncle Khairallah, after he was released from prison, who encouraged the boy to continue his education. Following his expulsion from the army, Khairallah went into education and rose to become a school head-master. Saddam is reported to have claimed in later years that his uncle was his ideal intellectual, the man who showed him the true value of education. Yet Khairallah seems to have taught his nephew lessons in ruthlessness, bigotry and manipulation, vital tools which Saddam later employed as he sought power in the complex politics of Iraq.[22]

A chilling but revealing insight into the thinking of Saddam's uncle-mentor may be derived from a volume published by the Iraqi state press after Saddam became president. This book, which laid out Khairallah's philosophical thoughts, was entitled: 'Three whom God should not have created: Persians, Jews, and Flies'. In it Khairallah defines Persians as 'animals God created in the shape of humans' and Jews as 'a mixture of the dirt and the leftovers of diverse peoples'. As for flies, although they are less appealing, no one can properly understand why they were created.[23] This quotation is important for it reflects the thinking of Saddam's earliest role model, and is a possible source for his lifelong attitude toward his enemies.

Another early influence on Saddam's thinking is said to have been Sami Shaukat, a nationalist intellectual who published *The Art of Death* in the 1930s. In Shaukat's words:

Strength means to excel in the art of death.
The nation which does not excel in the art of death with iron
    and fire
Will die under the horses' hooves, and under the boots of
    foreign soldiers.

Let us sanctify death by killing and sacrificing ourselves for the
  sake of the country.
Let us bow humbly before the art of death.[24]

The leader of Iraq has taken every opportunity to emphasise how
important education has been to his career, and to boast about his
knowledge and the breadth of his reading. He has claimed that works
of political thought and ideology are very important and interesting to
him. The memoirs of the revolutionary Colonel Salah al-Din al-Sabagh,
for example, were of particular interest to Saddam, since, despite his
ultimate failure, the colonel was 'a great nationalist who tried to achieve
Pan-Arab objectives'.[25] In addition, the books of Stalin were among
those Saddam read during his imprisonment.

More recently Saddam has shown a great interest in the Mafia, as
exemplified by the Mafia leader Don Corleone, portrayed in Saddam's
favourite movie, The Godfather, which he is believed to have seen many
times. The Iraqi leader's fascination with Don Corleone is explained
plausibly by Miller and Mylroie:

> The iron-willed character of the Don may perhaps be the most telling
> model for the enigmatic figure that rules Iraq. Both come from dirt
> poor peasant villages; both sustain their authority by violence and for
> both, family is key, the key to power. Family is every thing. ... Saddam,
> like the Godfather, ultimately trusts no one, not even his next of kin.
> For both, calculation and discipline, loyalty and ruthlessness are the
> measure of man's character.[26]

Saddam Hussein has rarely travelled outside the Middle East, con-
fining his official visits to places exclusively within the Arab world. His
only known trip to the West was to Paris in the mid-1970s. His lack of
familiarity with the most basic aspects of Western life has been revealed
in several television interviews with Western journalists. During one
interview, conducted before the Iraqi invasion of Kuwait, he tried to
explain and defend an Iraqi law that virtually allowed the execution of
anyone who dared to make jokes at the expense of the president. He
asked the bewildered ABC television correspondent Diane Sawyer,
'Doesn't the law in your country punish whoever tries to insult the
president?' She replied that if that were the case 'half of the country
would be in prison,' and that no such law existed. His response was to

take refuge in the lofty observation that 'in Iraq the president is regarded by the people as a symbol representing something.'[27]

On one of the rare occasions when he was humble enough to admit his ignorance, during an interview before the Gulf conflict, he asked an Arab journalist exactly how the US government functioned. When the journalist suggested that it would take a long time to explain, the president of Iraq asked him if he had a more important appointment. The journalist conceded that he probably did not, and carefully described the US government's system of checks and balances, and the all-important separation of executive, legislative and judicial functions. Saddam asked scornfully: 'Who, then am I supposed to deal with?'[28] Statements of this kind, although superficially unimportant, underline Saddam's extraordinary, not to say dangerous unfamiliarity with the sophisticated political system of the most powerful nation in the globe, a country he was nevertheless about to defy.

Saddam's Political Career

According to Saddam Hussein himself, the most important decision in his life was the one in 1955 that took him to Baghdad, where he attended school. Inspired by the example of Egypt's General Nasser, the mood in Baghdad in the mid-1950s was one of militant Arab nationalism. Not only was the newly-formed state of Israel arousing deep Arab resentment but the Baghdad Pact with Britain had just been signed. Cited by the Western-oriented Iraqi government of the day as an effort to stem the tide of Soviet communist expansion, it was interpreted by Arab nationalists as colonialism in a new guise. Nasser's response, in 1956, was to nationalise the Suez Canal. French, British, and Israeli forces then occupied the canal area but were forced by international pressure, particularly from the USA, to back down. Nasser emerged from the Suez military confrontation as a hero, the man who single-handedly had defied the imperialist powers. It is worth noting here that it was principally US pressure, under the leadership of President Dwight D. Eisenhower, which caused the British, the French, and the Israelis unconditionally to withdraw their military forces, thereby saving Nasser from an unavoidable and humiliating defeat.

While Nasser was successfully establishing himself in Egypt as the Arab nationalist David who routed the imperialist Goliath, Iraq under

King Feisal was perceived as reactionary and totally out of step with Arab aspirations. During this extraordinary post-Suez period, lit by the flames of an incipient Arab nationalism, Saddam Hussein was politically 'born' at the age of twenty as opposition in Iraq to Feisal's rule increased.[29] In July 1958, the king was overthrown in a bloody coup in which he, his brother and the prime minister were all shot and killed, thus ending the rule of the Hashemite dynasty. King Feisal was replaced by Brigadier General Abdul Karim Qassim. The body of the king, along with that of his prime minister Nuri al-Said, was taken from the palace, mutilated, dragged through the streets of Baghdad and finally strung up on a rope. Anarchic events such as these must have provided the young Saddam with dramatic first-hand evidence of the fate that awaited leaders in Iraq when they took chances with the security of their regime: it meant tampering with their own survival.

Saddam was soon accepted into the Ba'th party. His main credential for acceptance was his participation in a failed assassination attempt, when he and five others were given the task of killing the Iraqi prime minister. Abdul Karim Qassim survived. According to Saddam's official biographers, the young man had been so eager to rid the country of its brutal dictator that he forgot his role in the operation.[30] Saddam was wounded, but escaped across the Syrian border, where one of his comrades was able, by following his instructions as he watched bravely, to remove the bullet with a pair of scissors. This story has added much to the myth of his courage among the Iraqi population.[31]

The Ba'th leaders gave him a hero's welcome in Damascus. His official biography records when he met the co-founder and chief ideologue of the Ba'th party, Michel Aflaq, for the first time. Aflaq promoted Saddam to full membership in the party. This was a rare honour for a young peasant, and proved to be the turning point in his career. Unable to return to Iraq, he sought refuge in Egypt, where he completed his high school education in 1961. He enrolled in law school, but two years later political developments in Iraq interrupted his course of study. In 1963, General Qassim was ousted from power by a coalition of the Ba'th party and a group of Nasserite army officers. With the Ba'th party in power, Saddam quickly took the opportunity to return to Iraq. He did not in fact gain his degree until 1970, by which time he was already one step away from the Iraqi presidency.

Saddam made good use of the intervening seven years. Upon his arrival early in 1963, he found Iraq in political chaos. This both provided an outlet for his overweening ambitions, and suited the ruthless manipulative skills he had developed in his childhood. One of Saddam's first steps was to contract an advantageous marriage, to his cousin, the sister of an already popular public figure, Adnan Khairallah, who was later to become his defence minister.

The young Saddam began his early career in the Ba'th party as one of its leading assassins. Through his Takriti contacts, he was secretly promoted to the Regional Command Council and put in charge of a special force responsible for 'terror and assassination'.[32] The Ba'th party remained in control for only nine months, however, and when it fell from power, Saddam went underground. Following a failed coup d'état attempt, he was rounded up with many others and imprisoned. According to Saddam himself, while in prison he spent much time contemplating the Ba'th party's failure to retain power and planning for the future. In order to better understand the true nature of revolution, he says, he studied books on Lenin.[33]

His prison contemplation and study left him convinced that the Ba'th failure stemmed from disunity among its members. After leaving prison Saddam concentrated on building an internal security organisation capable of ensuring future loyalty through fear if not through shared belief or commitment. Employing all the security and intelligence expertise he had amassed, he created Jihaz Haneen, a disciplined and ruthless fighting force, and started building and cultivating cells of fanatics owing allegiance only to himself. When the Ba'th party eventually regained power in 1968, their loyalty was assured: they followed him, and him alone. Their leader was Saddam Hussein, whose political and military vision by now dominated every aspect of their thinking.[34]

Iraq's new leader, President al-Bakr, was a fellow Takriti and a relative of Saddam Hussein. The new president entrusted Saddam with the task of ensuring at all costs that the Ba'th party stayed in power this time. He also announced publicly what had been a secret: Saddam's full membership in the Revolutionary Command Council (RCC), by then the highest decision-making institution in the Ba'th party. In the years to follow, when treasonable plots were uncovered, whether real or imagined, it was Saddam Hussein who was seen in public ordering the execution of large numbers of people. In 1969, Saddam was rewarded for his service and became Assistant Secretary General of the Ba'th party and Deputy Chairman of the RCC.[35]

Saddam Hussein's rise to power in Iraq came as Nasser's life was drawing to a close. Saddam saw himself as the direct and logical successor to Egypt's president as the Arab world's leading political figure, and prepared to take up the torch of Arab nationalism when Nasser laid it down. Nasser was the twentieth century leader who most influenced and inspired Saddam Hussein's political career, as well as his political rhetoric. When Saddam was forced into exile in Egypt in the late 1950s, following his failed attempt upon the life of the Iraqi prime minister, he was able to observe first hand the workings of the Nasserite regime. In general he admired Nasser and was fascinated by what Nasser used to call 'reiterating the trial and error,' a method of determining policy that he later tried to follow.[36] According to his official biography, he was willing to criticise what he saw as Nasser's shortcomings, and instead of following him blindly, was able to learn both from Nasser's successes and from his failures.

Ironically, Saddam seems to have learned very little. Soon after the 1967 Egyptian defeat at the hands of Israel, for example, Nasser took the unusual step of accepting full personal responsibility for the disaster and announced his resignation. It was not until millions of his supporters had taken to the streets demanding that he stay in office that he reversed his decision. Twenty years later, Saddam, by contrast, having subjected his country to a costly eight-year war against Iran, with no clear objective and neither moral nor material gain, simply announced a reconciliation with Iran. In the process, he shelved the issue of the Shatt al-Arab waterway, which had been an original pretext for entering the war against Iran. Two years after this, he plunged his country into yet another devastating conflict.

After Iraq's humiliating defeat at the hands of the international coalition in 1991, many expected Saddam either to commit suicide or seek exile, or at least resign and leave a relative or subordinate to take over. Instead, Saddam blamed others for the defeat, denied all personal responsibility, clung to power and continued his defiance in the face of crippling international sanctions, which held his country hostage. This was not the only difference between Nasser and Saddam. Unlike Nasser, who was considered one of the greatest orators in modern Arab history, Saddam is 'not a great orator and his speeches are short and rare. His press conferences are even less frequent.'[37] Nasser's speeches concerned issues relevant to the humblest of his listeners, couched in simple but inspirational language, and were impatiently awaited by the masses throughout the Arab world.[38] Saddam, by contrast, uses words in a grandiose manner, with intimidating, elitist language intended to 'instil order, calculation and prudence into the volatile minds of the Iraqi masses'. Ironically, for him, according to one observer, 'time is better spent in thinking and rethinking, relearning and silently working, and he has a great deal to do of all of that.' The weakness of his political oratory is well captured in the following excerpt from one of his speeches:

> We are still within the stage of calculation of mere aspirations; we are still at the beginning of the road which we have resolved to cover: the road towards the building of socialism, the defeat of imperialism and the creation of this country as a safe base for Arab struggle in general and a model experiment illuminating the entire region of the Middle East.[39]

There is one further, very significant difference between the two leaders – Nasser's international orientation, compared to Saddam's narrower domestic political concerns. Early on in his career, Nasser understood the unique international role granted to Egypt by her geographical position. As he pointed out in his popular book, *The Philosophy of the Revolution*, which was published in 1954, Egypt lies within, and can influence, three concentric cultural circles – Arab, Islamic, and African. Thus the Egyptian leader, a sophisticated internationalist, constantly sought to maintain his country's position as an influential, autonomous nation able to play a significant mediating role in the Middle East. In sharp contrast, the Iraqi leader's first concern has always been to suppress his internal enemies.[40]

Saddam did not become politically visible until he was admitted as a member of the RCC in 1969. His debt to President al-Bakr, therefore, is enormous. The two men were united by more than simply their Takrit background and Ba'th ideology. They belonged to the same tribe, and were closely related. As the historian Hanna Batatu points out, 'Saddam is the foster-son, nephew and son-in-law of Khairallah [who is the] second cousin of al-Bakr. It is partly upon this relationship that Saddam's political position rests.'[41]

Saddam's first task, as President al-Bakr's relative and security chief, was to suppress any possibility of a counter-revolutionary plot. In this context he perceived the newly-appointed prime minister, Razaq Nayef, as a major threat, and in a bold but vintage Saddam move he forced Nayef at gun-point to accompany him to the airport, where an aeroplane was waiting to take him into forced exile. Ten years later, in order no doubt further to reinforce Saddam's position, Nayef was assassinated in London by the Mukhabarat, the Iraqi secret police.

Thus the nature and organisational style of Saddam Hussein's political career was established. At that time, President al-Bakr presented the moderate, acceptable public face of the Ba'th party while Vice-President Saddam Hussein ensured, by whatever means necessary, that the regime stayed in power. Internal security and the enlarging of the numbers of the party membership were his main interests. This two-pronged leadership arrangement continued for nearly a decade, during which time President al-Bakr placed growing numbers of his and Saddam's relatives and trusted comrades in positions of administrative importance. But the time came when Saddam, whose political career had been enormously assisted by al-Bakr, would no longer be satisfied with his position as second-in-command.

The exact circumstances surrounding his take-over of power remain obscure. On 16 July 1979, however, President al-Bakr made a televised speech in which he announced his retirement from the presidency 'for reasons of health'. Thus, al-Bakr clearly made a public show of resigning willingly, even though it is believed that his resignation was forced on him. In his acceptance speech the following day, as President of the Republic of Iraq, Saddam Hussein showed his political hand:

> It has never happened before, either in ancient history (including that of our nation since its dawn) or in modern times, that two leaders have been in power for eleven years within one command, without this resulting in a dangerous moral or practical imbalance in leadership, and without their relationship ending in one of them driving the other out.[42]

Saddam had bludgeoned his way to the top by means of ruthless opportunism, making and breaking alliances when expedient, and purging actual or potential rivals via trumped-up charges and the firing squad.[43] And once his *de facto* presidency became official, he wasted no time before openly and decisively taking steps to annihilate his few remaining rivals. Eleven days after he assumed the presidency, he announced that his security forces had uncovered a plot against the state – a plot that he described as having 'foreign backing,' a clear reference to his rival, the Ba'th party of Syria. The alleged plot was found to implicate hundreds of potentially uncooperative party members, army officers and old friends and colleagues, 22 of whom were publicly executed by firing squad in the presence of Saddam and his cabinet members.[44]

This dramatic action allowed Saddam to take revenge on old enemies, rid himself of all high-ranking party members who were not unreservedly his supporters, and at the same time rally the country around him in a show of unity that served to consolidate his power. There was some speculation that a union had been seriously proposed between the Ba'th parties of Syria and Iraq, with Samarrai, an old political rival of Saddam's, as the president of Iraq – and, indeed, Samarrai was one of those executed. The 'plot' gave Saddam a free hand to set the political tone of his administration. Having pensioned off his principal benefactor, a man regarded by his people as their 'father' (al-Bakr died in retirement two years later), he then brought about the violent deaths of all those likely to oppose his objectives. Saddam Hussein, these actions suggest, is a man who understands politics entirely in the Hobbesian sense, as an activity to be detached from all emotion.

The wholesale liquidation of his rivals was an undertaking that was not without risk for Saddam. It left no possibility, however, that others might mistake his capacities or his intentions. Furthermore, by coercing his colleagues into participation in the killings, Saddam wove a fabric of collective guilt, a public sharing of responsibility that enabled him to call the killings 'democratic execution'. Most important of all, Saddam was able from the outset to set a violent political tone for the government of the entire nation, and to present himself as the un-challenged leader of his army, his party, and his people.

The Politics of the Image

Saddam Hussein has made a calculated use of popular image-building in his single-minded quest for power. Principally he has sought to create a belief in his superhuman qualities in his own people's minds. A particularly revealing episode relates to a film made in Iraq that depicts his participation in the assassination attempt on Qassim, in the course of which he was shot in the leg. In an interview with Saddam, the scene showing the removal of the bullet from his leg prompted an Egyptian journalist to offer discreet advice. He approved of the film in every respect, except 'when your comrade [an actor] cuts into your leg, using a razor blade to get a bullet out. The actor who was playing your part only grimaces.' The journalist's suggestion was that the actor 'should scream in pain. It would be more realistic [and also would] show people that you, as a human being, have physically suffered.' 'I did not think it was realistic either,' the Iraqi president answered. 'I wanted the director to re-shoot the scene because I remember the day when it happened. I did not grimace or move an inch until the bullet was out.'[45]

The myth of the great leader is promoted vigorously; statues and cut-out figures are found throughout the streets of Baghdad and in every town throughout Iraq. Saddam's overwhelming power is omni-present – and is most visible in a 13-metre high portrait in the centre of Baghdad. His portrait can be seen in every shop, school, police station, and public building, and behind every official desk.[46]

Saddam also recognises the symbolic power of the soldier over the civilian. Thus, although he is not a member of the Iraqi army, has received no army training, and holds no army rank, he is frequently depicted in military uniform and is known for his fondness for military metaphors in his speeches. He may well thus be compensating for his lack of a genuine military background, since very few members of his cabinet have no service connections. The contrast with President Nasser is again interesting. A trained army officer with long years of experience, Nasser nevertheless abandoned his military uniform when he assumed the presidency.

Along with his identity as a super-human military leader, Saddam Hussein possesses multitudinous official titles, more than any other leader in recent memory. Al-Khalil lists some of the more important: President of the Republic, Chairman of the Council of Ministers, Commander-in-Chief of the Armed Forces, Chairman of the RCC, General Secretary of the Regional Command of the Arab Ba'th Socialist Party, Chairman of the Supreme Planning Council, Chairman

of the Committee on Agreements, Chairman of the Supreme Agri-
cultural Council and Chairman of the Supreme Council for the
Compulsory Eradication of Illiteracy. In addition, he carries honorific
titles which have been devised exclusively for his use. Thus, he is Iraq's
Leader-President, the Leader-Struggler, the Standard Bearer, the Arab
Leader, the Knight of the Arab Nation, the Hero of the National
Liberation, the Father-Leader and the Daring and Aggressive Knight.[47]

Like other narcissistic leaders who have identified with famous world
figures, Saddam has many heroes. These include Gandhi, Lenin, Nasser,
de Gaulle, Che Guevara, Tito, Castro, and Ali bin Abi Talib. Each
man seems to exemplify for Saddam a single characteristic or virtue –
courage, ruthlessness, patriotism – and that may be why he needs so
many. His single most important exemplar, however, is Nebuchadnezzar
(605 to 562 BC), an Arab political administrator (a king in the Bible)
who conquered Jerusalem and destroyed its temple. Nebuchadnezzar
conceived and built the hanging gardens of Babylon in Baghdad, a
magnificent architectural undertaking which Saddam vainly attempted
to rebuild himself at a very high cost. It was under King Nebuchadnezzar that fighting first began between Persians and Arabs, a conflict
that in one form or another has continued ever since.[48] In a rare
moment of quiet reflection, when asked why his admiration of Nebuchadnezzar was so strong, Saddam replied:

> Nebuchadnezzar stirs in me everything relating to pre-Islamic ancient
> history. I am reminded that any human being with broad horizons,
> faith and feeling can act wisely but practically, attain his goals and
> become a great man who makes his country into a great state. And
> what is most important to me about Nebuchadnezzar is the link
> between the Arabs' abilities and the liberation of Palestine. Nebuchad-
> nezzar was after all an Arab from Iraq, albeit ancient Iraq.
> Nebuchadnezzar was the one who brought the bound Jewish slaves
> from Palestine. That is why whenever I remember [him] I like to
> remind the Arabs, Iraqis in particular, of their historical respons-
> ibilities. It is a burden that should not stop them from action, but
> rather spur them into action because of their history.[49]

In addition to needing great heroes in metaphor, Saddam has also
sought genuine blood ties with nobility. Whether this is a personal need
or a response to a wish to bolster his legitimacy in other parts of the
Arab world,[50] Saddam has claimed to be a descendant of the Imam

Ali, the fourth Caliph, who was a companion of the Prophet. He has issued a new family tree which traces his ancestry to this patron of the Shi'a sect. Although this may appear to be merely a political move, designed to associate him with the Iraqi Shi'a majority, al-Khalil argues to the contrary: 'It signified contempt for the populace, large numbers of whom he knew would accept this proof of ancestry, largely because there was no longer a soul in the length and breadth of the country who could be heard if they were prepared to deny it.'[51]

Yet Saddam himself appears to believe in his newly-acquired nobility, if his deliberately offensive letter to the president of Egypt immediately after the invasion of Kuwait is anything to judge by.

> The speaker himself … came from a noble family whose prime honour lay in its work, and in that it descended from the Quraishi Mohammed family to which the Imam al-Hussein, our forefather, the son of Imam Ali bin Abi Talib belonged. To my knowledge, Your Excellency, you are from an Egyptian family that is not related to princes or kings.[52]

Another intriguing historical influence on Saddam is believed to stem from his fascination with a seventh century Islamic leader, al-Hajaj al-Thaqafi. Appointed governor of Kufa and Basra by Abd al-Malik bin Marwan, the Ummayyad Caliph, al-Hajaj, was sent to quell the disturbances there. He ordered the execution of all dissidents, beheading them and displaying their heads in public (a practice that Saddam would later employ himself). Going straight to the mosque for his first address to his subjects soon after his arrival, al-Hajaj gave a fiery and memorable speech:

> I am the son of splendour, the scaler of high places. When I take off my turban you know who I am. By God, I shall make evil bear its own burden … I see heads before me that are ripe and ready for plucking, and I am the one to pluck them, and I see blood glistening between the turbans and the beards … By God, O People of Iraq, people of discord and dissembling and evil character! I can not be squeezed like a fig or scared like a camel … My powers have been tested and my experience proved and I pursue my aim to the end … By God I shall strip you like bark, I shall truss you like a bundle of twigs, I shall beat you like stray camels... Indeed you are like a people of 'a village which was safe and calm, its sustenance coming in plenty from every side, and they denied the grace of God, and God let them

taste the garment of hunger and of fear for what they had done' ...
I swear by God that you will keep strictly to the true path, or I shall
punish every man of you in his body.[53]

This speech is memorised by every Iraqi student, as it is considered
an important part of classical Arabic literature; it is cited by writers to
describe the exercise of absolute power in tyrannical states. It also had
another function, in that it served as a fearsome tool for cultivating and
massaging young Iraqi minds.

The politics of the image wields great influence in Iraq and is crudely
imposed upon its people. Saddam Hussein's birthday, for example, has
become a national holiday: the whole country is obliged to celebrate
the day its dictator was born. Each year he links his birthday with a
different historical figure. During the 1990 crisis, Saddam chose as his
exemplar Sargon the Great (2300 BC), a victorious leader well-known
to Iraqis, who won all his battles.[54] Whether or not the Iraqi people
accepted the imagery is hard to say. In a police state, cheering crowds
outside a palace are no reliable indicator.

Saddam: The Political Practitioner

Following his ruthless purge of opposition upon coming to power,
Saddam was free to embark on his own political agenda. This proved
to be a campaign with three main goals, described by the writer Amatzia
Baram as increasing Iraq's influence in the Third World, enhancing his
personal position, and strengthening his claim to the leadership of the
Arab world.[55] His role model, as noted above, was the late Gamal Abdel
Nasser of Egypt, whose death left a leadership vacuum in the Arab
world that Saddam hoped to fill.

Egypt lost its central influence and leadership role in Arab politics
when it signed the Camp David peace agreement with Israel. This gave
Saddam Hussein the opportunity to be at the forefront of the subsequent campaign to expel Egypt from the Arab League. Strengthened
by Iraq's rising oil revenues – political upheavals in Iran had caused
international panic and sent oil prices rocketing – Saddam was able to
threaten dire consequences to any Arab nation rash enough to support
Egypt.

In Saddam Hussein's political thinking, Baghdad is the natural centre
for Arab political unity. 'We must make this country the solid base and

living pillar of the whole Arab struggle, an example which will shine throughout the Middle East,' he declared in a speech in 1974.[56] Saddam emphasises that Iraq's development is the *sine qua non* for any wider Arab advancement. No sooner did he assume the presidency in 1979 than he declared in his first speech that:

> The glory of Arabs stems from the glory of Iraq. Throughout history, whenever Iraq became mighty and flourished, so did the Arab Nation. This is why we are striving to make Iraq mighty, formidable, able and developed, and why we shall spare nothing to improve the welfare and to brighten the glory of Iraqis.[57]

In a later interview, he elaborated on his vision of one Arab nation based on a strong Iraq, and how it could be accomplished:

> Iraq today, with its principles, is an extraordinary power within the nation. Yet its power is not sufficient if it is only surrounded by weak regions. It can most certainly help in the development of the nation, through the power invested in it by the principles of the party. Iraq can assist in the strengthening of other regions in the Arab nation, both directly and indirectly.[58]

In the same interview, Saddam expressed his dissatisfaction with the status of his country as a 'developing' nation and described how he intended to help it to catch up with the developed world. An increase in per capita income was the key.[59] He admitted, however, that he was 'constantly disturbed by one thought: finding ourselves at a point when our reserves are exhausted ... without having a flourishing agricultural sector or a sound infrastructure. We would then have condemned ourselves to an eternal state of underdevelopment.'[60]

Saddam shows no interest in ideas of freedom and democracy. In an interview with Majid Khadduri, when Saddam was questioned about his people's freedom, he said that the country should not expect such achievements overnight: 'Most difficult of all is to achieve freedom and democracy,' with the clear implication that these should defer to what he went on to describe as more important issues.[61] On the occasion of probably the most democratic recent development in Iraq, the creation of the national assembly, Saddam uncompromisingly spelled out his views on democracy: 'We hope and must assure that the 13 million [Iraqis] walk the same road. He who takes the crooked path, will meet the sword.'[62]

In an interview soon afterwards, when Saddam was asked why the Iraqi Ba'th official party slogan (Unity, Freedom, and Socialism) did not follow that of Egypt (Freedom, Socialism, and Unity), he replied:

> The Arabs must struggle for a national truth; they cannot achieve true liberty without nationalism and the struggle towards Arab unity ... It means that the party's program is based on the fact that an Arab must be a nationalist to achieve true liberty. This must ultimately lead to unity and from there to socialism.[63]

Nasser attempted to rule by communicating to and relating directly with people, their daily concerns and their daily needs. Saddam on the other hand, rules through political jargon, grandiose myths, and a focus on issues of 'high politics'. In particular, he inspires them with his dream of an Arab state with its past glories regained, a state the equal of any other in the world. This dream is to be realised, though he does not explicitly say so, through the costly acquisition of high technology, the creation of a vast army, and the rule of terror.[64] Arab unity under his leadership will begin in Iraq, and will not depend so much upon the people's choice – democratic politics – as upon the accumulation of sufficient wealth to impose it, through a form of capitalist economics. Saddam's invasion of Kuwait, therefore, fits into a cherished long-term goal: the imposition of his hegemony on the entire region. Not only might it have been the first step toward an enforced political unity, it could also have brought vast and much-needed wealth with it as well. Darwish and Alexander believe that an Iraqi plan to subjugate the Gulf states was worked out during the war with Iran. The US Department of State has also concluded that the invasion was 'a long-term plan and part of Saddam's bid to lead the Arab world on his own terms and in his own Ba'th style to subject the Gulf states'.[65]

The Iraqi invasion of Iran in 1980 could also be seen as part of Saddam's long-term plans for strengthening his political position in the region. A defeated and humiliated Iran, possibly with 'Arabistan' (the Arabic speaking region in Iran) carved off and joined to Iraq, would have eliminated a major external threat to Iraq, and would have enhanced Saddam's political and military stature not only in the Arab world but far beyond.

In the uneasy period of peace between the end of the war with Iran and the Iraqi invasion of Kuwait, Saddam engaged in a politically high-profile exercise in regional alliance-building. In February 1989, he convinced Jordan, Egypt and Yemen that they should enter into a formal agreement to create the Arab Co-operation Council (ACC). Since the Gulf Co-operation Council (GCC), which had been formed in 1980 (when Iraq was preoccupied with the war with Iran), included only six oil-rich Gulf countries, the ACC was perceived by its members as a necessary regional grouping, established solely for the purposes of economic co-operation.

The ACC agreement was designed to serve Saddam's purposes. In particular it sent usefully different messages to different parties. To Western observers, Iraq's participation in an economic bloc that included Egypt and Jordan seemed to signify a new Iraqi phase of political pragmatism after its crippling war of attrition against Iran. The agreement also could be seen as belated vengeance against the 'rich club' of the GCC, and therefore was of great satisfaction to the poorer countries, Egypt, Jordan and Yemen. Furthermore Saddam could now count more than ever on the Yemenis' support against the Saudis. Less than two months after the ACC agreement, King Fahd signed a non-aggression pact with Iraq. The nature of this perplexing accord between Saudi Arabia and the untrustworthy Saddam was best captured in Britain's *Financial Times*: 'If Margaret Thatcher were to show up ... in Paris and sign a non-aggression pact ... people would think it more than a little odd.'[66] It is reported that when King Fahd expressed surprise at Saddam's overtures, the Iraqi leader claimed that there had been rumours to the effect that Saudi Arabia was plotting against Iraq and that by signing the pact, the king would be refuting them.[67]

Saddam's domestic and foreign policies have both been characterised by opportunism. He has made concessions when these have been to his immediate advantage, but has not hesitated to break agreements when it suits him at a later stage.

One of the greatest threats to the stability of modern Iraq has been the unresolved problem of the Iraqi Kurds. With an estimated population of approximately two and a half million, the Sunni-Muslim Kurds mostly inhabit the oil-rich north and north-east of Iraq.[68] Once the Ba'th party had come to power, the Kurds became its most pressing security issue. Not only was the Kurdish national movement well organised and militarily well equipped, but it was ready and willing, even eager, to be made use of by nations hostile to Iraq, such as Iran or Turkey. Quick to sense the Kurdish danger and its possible outcome, Saddam moved promptly, luring the leader of the Kurdish movement into signing a profoundly disadvantageous cease-fire agreement. The importance of this agreement (which appeared to promise Kurdish autonomy) to the government in Baghdad is well described by Batatu: '[The] most pressing danger was the restlessness of the Kurds. The agreement of March 11, 1970, with their veteran leader Mulla Mustafa al-Barazani, providing for their autonomy in the areas in which they form a majority, proved, while it lasted, a shot in the arm of the government.' [69]

Typical of Saddam's early deceit in the practice of politics, as the Kurds soon discovered to their bitter disgust, the implementation of the Autonomy Law for the Region of Kurdistan, to which he had agreed, in effect expired the very day it was signed. The Israeli journalist Uriel Dann explains the legal loophole Saddam persuaded the trusting, tribalistic Kurds to accept: 'The execution of the law was left to the discretion of the central government from whose decisions there lay no appeal. Political and security affairs ominously came under its sole jurisdiction.'[70]

Iran, a traditional Iraqi enemy, represented a further threat to the stability of Saddam's administration. The Shah of Iran consistently added to the insecurity of the region by doing everything in his power to assist the Iraqi Kurds and to discourage any reconciliation between them and their Arab co-nationalists. In 1969, he declared null and void the 1937 treaty which had in effect given Iraq control of the Shatt al-Arab waterway. He also continually encouraged Iraqi right-wingers to overthrow their government. Furthermore, in his efforts to become a major power in the Middle East, from 1974 onwards the Shah went on an armaments spending spree, buying roughly $3.5 billion worth in that first year.

Faced with this clear threat, in 1975 Saddam once again saw discretion as the better part of valour. In Algiers, he and the shah, his most bitter enemy, signed an agreement which stipulated that the two countries would cease all subversive political activities against each other. This relatively meaningless accord eased the threat on Saddam's northern border and made it possible for him to devote most of his resources to dealing a final blow to Iraq's indigenous Kurds.

One of Saddam's most important contributions to his country's foreign policy was his work toward a rapprochement with the USSR, which eventually led to the Treaty of Friendship and Co-operation on 9 April 1972. He was the point man who negotiated with Kosygin, won concessions the Soviets rarely granted, and seems to have been the main driving force behind the treaty.[71] Not only did it provide Iraq with much-needed military hardware to counter-balance the growing strength of Iran, but it guaranteed assistance in the fields of both technology and economics.[72] This Soviet support also gave Saddam a significant psychological advantage. The looming threat of a Russian presence in the Middle East not only made the West uneasy; the Gulf nations also felt intimidated, and with good reason.

Eventually, however, when the Russians had outlasted their usefulness, the pragmatic Saddam adroitly created a crisis in which he was able to purge his own Iraqi Communists and to accuse the Russians of being 'insensitive,' in that 'they would not be satisfied until the whole world turned communist'. He was also, in a quintessentially Saddam move, one of the first Middle East leaders to condemn the Soviet invasion of Afghanistan.

But first, with the opening he had gained from his uneasy rapprochement with the Shah of Iran, he was able to use Soviet aid to great advantage in the war with the Kurds which had flared up the moment they fully realised how they had been betrayed. In short, Saddam had proved himself to be a master in manipulating the Soviet Union's patronage, and eventually had turned what they had thought of as an asset into a decided liability.

Another highlight of Saddam's rule in Iraq within the sphere of Arab politics came immediately after the signing of the Camp David agreement. During the politically tense period following Israel and Egypt's agreement to a peace settlement, pressure was exerted upon Saddam to counter Sadat with some meaningful political initiative. Saddam responded by convening a special emergency meeting of the Arab League in the Iraqi capital, denouncing the treaty and applying political and economic measures that effectively boycotted Egypt.

This was insufficient to calm Arab fears of what might happen next, however, given the power of the new USA/Israel/Egypt axis created at Camp David. It seemed obvious that Syria and Iraq, the two champions of the Arab cause, would forget their ideological differences. Syria, although reluctant, was willing to do so. The Iraqi government, on the other hand, was divided: President al-Bakr signalled his willingness to co-operate with Syria, but Saddam Hussein, the *de facto* president, was bitterly opposed to the idea and unleashed a virulent attack on Syria through the state-controlled newspapers.[73]

It was against this background that Saddam forced President al-Bakr, his relative and former friend, to retire. As noted above, this step gave Saddam a free hand, which he used immediately to purge all Iraqi supporters of the proposed unity with Syria under the pretext of a Syrian-backed plot to overthrow the Iraqi government. Saddam's accession to power, furthermore, went a long way toward calming the fears raised in Arab minds by the Camp David treaty. He was a leader Arabs could respect, if not always trust.

It was this Middle East perception that gave Saddam *carte blanche* to pursue his political ambitions. Even so, his invasion of Iran in 1980, clearly encouraged by his belief that Iran's military forces had been seriously weakened during the revolution against the shah, was a dangerous miscalculation. Iran's population is three times larger than Iraq's and its land mass is much bigger. In addition, although Iran was still in political chaos following the overthrow of its ruling dynasty, a shrewder opponent than Saddam might have realised that what Iran most needed was an external villain, someone or something to divert the people's attention from its internal political and economic problems. In fact, as the Iraqi invasion gave Iranian religious fervour a focus and an outlet, that is exactly what happened. Iraq as a result got bogged down in one of the most ferocious wars of attrition in the period since the Second World War. The war was to continue for eight years and claim over a million lives, depleting Iraqi cash reserves. In this author's opinion, it gave Saddam Hussein no alternative but to attempt to take over Kuwait, with the resulting political and economic morass, and disaster for Iraq.

With Saddam's accession to power, his personal ideology was seen most clearly in his promotion of the Non-Aligned Movement, with the idea that Iraq might be its leading member-state. Iraqi participation arose from a commitment rooted in *raison d'état* to 'progressive' and 'national liberation' movements in general.[74] In fact Saddam's over-riding concerns may well have been economic. Steven Bashkett, for one, argues that by pursuing the policy of non-alignment, Iraq improved its image abroad and so was able to acquire armaments and advanced technology that otherwise would have been forbidden it. Also, by advocating issues favourable to the interests of the Third World, Iraq may appear to have gained little, but in fact it 'enhances its image and minimises the likelihood of a Third World backlash against the disproportionate power and wealth of oil-rich states.'[75]

Saddam's Invasion of Kuwait

The decision to invade Kuwait was by far the most important the Iraqi leader has ever made. Its significance extends far beyond any risk to his career, or even to his person. The decision brought into question the future existence of Iraq and certainly the political and personal welfare of Saddam himself. The war and the destruction it brought upon Iraq have set that country's economic development back many years. The war in Kuwait also had an unprecedented international impact. The solid international coalition that was mobilised under the auspices of the United Nations was a new development in the international arena, and one that is sometimes cited as a standard by which to measure UN success and effectiveness. (Two contrasting cases are the UN's more recent failures in dealing with Israel over the issue of the Palestinian deportees, and with the Bosnian conflict.)

From the data now available, and in light of what is known from Saddam's own speeches, it appears that the invasion of Kuwait may have been contemplated by the Iraqi government over a lengthy period, but that the timing was entirely Saddam's responsibility. Chief among new sources of information is a book in Arabic entitled *Harb taled okhra* (War Delivers Another), written by Saad al-Bazzaz, who is known to be a close companion of Saddam, with access to powerful members of the Iraqi government. In the book he criticises the Iraqi leadership for poor organisation and a lack of sophistication in its dealings with the West. And although al-Bazzaz nowhere states unequivocally that Saddam was personally responsible for the invasion, the only clear inference to be drawn from his account of events is that responsibility for them must eventually rest upon the man who has declared himself to be the 'ultimate leader'.

Seeking to explain the precise timing of the invasion, and its extreme ferocity, al-Bazzaz points obliquely to the frustration and anger of the Iraqi leadership with the long and ultimately futile negotiations with

Kuwait to extract financial concessions. He blames the Kuwaiti press for inflaming the crisis by calling Saddam the 'Arabs' Ceausescu,' a reference to the Romanian dictator. While the conflict is considered by the author to have been primarily of an economic nature, other factors are also said to have infuriated Saddam and brought matters to a head. Among these was the behaviour of wealthy Kuwaitis flaunting their money during visits to Baghdad. Currency speculation was also an aggravating factor: the Iraqi dinar had tumbled against the Kuwaiti dinar over the past ten years, from 20-to-1 to 1-to-250.[76] And, in addition to his intransigence over contentious issues such as Iraq's oil debt and the Gulf islands, the Emir of Kuwait, almost alone among Arab leaders, declined to pay homage to Saddam after his 'victory' against Iran.

In a speech made to Arab heads of state in Baghdad, at the summit conference of May 1990, entitled 'Threats to Arab National Security,' Saddam accused the United States and Kuwait of orchestrating a campaign against Iraq that was economic, psychological and military. Saddam declared that there was no difference between an economic war and a war which used army weapons and destruction.[77] During the conference, he also complained bitterly about oil prices that, thanks to Kuwait, at one point had 'tumbled to seven dollars a barrel'. When al-Bazzaz asked Iraq's foreign minister, Tariq Aziz, if all possible solutions had been explored and exhausted, including a 'technical' one, similar to the Syrian action in Lebanon, Aziz temporised, and requested a clarification. Al-Bazzaz rephrased his question: since the quarrel with Kuwait could be perceived as a personal problem between the Kuwaiti and Iraqi leaders, why was it not sufficient to get rid of the leadership? The answer was, 'No, it had to be a strategic punch.'[78] The RCC on another occasion 'concluded the need immediately to find a different language in dealing with Kuwait'.[79] Al-Bazzaz further reveals for the first time that one reason for Iraq's increasingly aggressive rhetoric towards Israel and later toward Kuwait was the hope that the US Secretary of State would take Iraq seriously and travel to Baghdad to discuss the matter. Had the USA done that, al-Bazzaz asserts, the war would have been avoided.[80]

The prominent Egyptian intellectual Mohamed Heikal, in his book, *Illusions of Triumph*, analyses the reasons for Saddam's actions with understanding and even sympathy. A protégé of Nasser, who is also an influential and widely-read writer, Heikal persuasively argues that the escalation of the conflict – including the verbal attacks on Israel and the US before the invasion – was less a challenge to Washington or Tel Aviv than a deliberate excursion by Saddam intended to assert his dominance and regional leadership of the Arab world in the wake of the collapse of the Soviet Union.[81]

Heikal argues that the Iraqi leader genuinely believed that the USA, along with Britain and Israel, was involved in a plot to weaken or destroy Iraq. For example, the Voice of America spearheaded the US media's negative portrayal of the Iraqi president to an Arabic-speaking audience. In a meeting with US senators before the invasion, Saddam asked them angrily:

> Why is that we are treated this way in the Western media? The Arabs listen every day to the insults against them. Why have you allowed yourselves to be under the influence of Zionists and Zionist lobbies to this extent? Why? We want peace but we don't want to surrender. We don't want to go down on our knees ... The country which fought for eight years defending its dignity and territory is ready to continue and sacrifice more.[82]

The US State Department's annual human rights report directly criticised the regime – in particular over the use of poison gas against the Kurds. Later, the US Congress passed legislation halting any shipment of wheat to Iraq, while the British authorities held and confiscated a shipment which they claimed was for an Iraqi super-gun project. These actions, and many others, led Saddam Hussein to conclude that the West was hostile and would try to undermine Iraq's power.

Conclusion

The three principal causes of conflict outlined in the work of Thomas Hobbes – competition, self-defence (or the perception thereof), and glory – seem to underlie all the international and local political strategies of Saddam Hussein. Virtually all his political contributions to the state of Iraq have been inspired by his overriding need to prolong his personal survival or that of the Iraqi Ba'th party which he dominates.

For eleven years, Saddam Hussein patiently gave his respect and obedience to the only Iraqi political figure superior to him, al-Bakr. When he calculated that his patience was no longer necessary and that circumstances were in his favour, Saddam moved swiftly, forcing his friend and mentor into the oblivion of exile and cleansing Iraq's top echelon of all its 'undesirable' elements.

Saddam's use of political power shows little willingness to abide by previous commitments, when he perceives it to be in his interest to break them. Remembering his experience with the previous Ba'th failure, he initially negotiated a political settlement with the Kurds, but when he felt that Iraq's internal fabric was strong enough, he moved swiftly against them, reneging without compunction on the deal. Saddam's contempt for treaty obligations was shown again when, contrary to the agreement signed in Algiers in 1975, he invaded Iran. What mattered to Saddam was the principle of political self-preservation. When threatened, he felt it his duty to strike back with all the means at his disposal. He could not possibly remain silent in the face of Iranian provocations in 1980; likewise, the invasion of Kuwait was motivated not only by economic necessity but also by the need to maintain his own position as the glorious Arab hero. Both invasions give every sign of having been expressions of Saddam's narcissistic inferiority complex projected outwards. Iran and Kuwait were two countries which happened to have challenged his superiority – an action which, as a threat to his self-image, called for his retaliation at any cost.

Saddam Hussein is a leader with a complex personality. Partly, he remains the very young man who, growing up surrounded by domestic and social violence, in his turn is said to have bullied and terrified his neighbourhood. When he became the leader of Iraq, he employed the same crude methods to establish his authority – with more sophisticated weaponry. His ability to obtain and keep power in Iraq attests to his political skill. But, above all, it reflects the use of terror and the iron fist. Although he embarked upon some of the most ambitious economic programmes in the developing world, his distorted vision of his country's future resulted in a form of distorted development in the Soviet manner, based on military power. It is ironic that during the Gulf War, while the Soviet empire was crumbling and its satellite states were breaking and running, the Iraqi leader was sacrificing his country in the same outmoded style.

One of the most important characteristics of the Iraqi leader, however, is his fondness for the politics of contention and rivalry. He did not inherit his position or obtain it easily: it was his skilful use of alignments and, when necessary, total ruthlessness, that brought about his rise to the Iraqi presidency. Over his entire political career, Saddam has resorted to the most brutally competitive methods in his pursuit of power. His cut-throat instincts have been employed at the state level, where he has encouraged different factions and institutions to compete against one another, thereby facilitating their ultimate subordination to his will. His military invasions of his neighbours Iran and Kuwait are further examples of this competitive drive.

In his pursuit of ever-greater power, Saddam has constantly wooed his Arab neighbours, justifying his acts of aggression as necessary self-defence, an honourable response to the conspiracy around him. Thus, during the invasion of Kuwait he kept up a high level of accusations against other nations which he claimed were out to topple his regime. Similarly, during the war with Iran he invoked the traditional theme of Arab defence against Persian invaders. When the war ended, he turned to the Gulf countries and requested compensation from them for his defence of the 'Eastern Arab gate' against the Persians.

If violence is the hallmark of the Iraqi government under Saddam, glory for Iraq and indeed for the entire Arab world has been his tantalising ultimate goal. The appeal for Arabs to restore their past glory is his central theme, an emotive issue which understandably speaks powerfully to many Arabs. Glory is at the root, too, of Saddam Hussein's obsession with King Nebuchadnezzar and the days of Babylon.

Insecure, manipulative, power-hungry, ruthless, obsessed with glories past, present and future, Saddam Hussein's psychology is central to any understanding of his actions.

If, as cultural pattern theorists argue, individual personality is formed by the child's early contacts with his surroundings, the child consequently thinks, acts, and feels in culturally approved manners. Saddam's personality owes much to his childhood in a broken family, and his familiarity with violence at an early age. While Saddam's personality was one cause of the Gulf War, however, there were also other important causes. As Samir al-Khalil points out in his *Republic of Fear*, which attempts to explain Saddam in a larger context, the Iraqi leader's place in his own culture and his own history, and their place in him, are both highly significant. They will be examined in the next part of this book.

Chapter 3

The State of Iraq

Iraq is a state in which the sole ruler holds absolute power and is the object of a personality cult. At the same time it has adopted socialist economic policies and upholds the idea of egalitarian reform. Iraq, therefore, practises a combination of political repression and social reform in which programmes to promote literacy and education are not accompanied by any provision of freedom for political organisation or intellectual and political expression. The state's authority is based on Saddam Hussein, the military and the Ba'th party.

The structure of authority and power within Iraq, coupled with its underdeveloped infrastructure create the political instability which has drawn it into the two significant regional conflicts which have characterised Saddam Hussein's rule. We will now examine the formation and structure of the state of Iraq. Our point here will be to assess the contribution made by the distinctive characteristics of the Iraqi state to the course of events resulting in the invasion of Kuwait and the Gulf crisis of 1990–91.

Iraq is a nation state created in the twentieth century as part of a new political map of the Middle East drawn up by Britain and France after the First World War. As is the case with many such states, its population is not homogeneous, and its assigned borders have been considered disadvantageous by the various Iraqi state elites since independence. Iraq's population includes a diversity of religious sects, the most populous of which are Shi'a and Sunni Muslims. The country has one large non-Arab national minority, the Kurds. The fear of Kurdish secession has been a constant preoccupation of recent Iraqi governments.

Contemporary Iraq has been shaped by the rule of the Ba'th party. Iraq is a one-party state whose government has engaged in extensive

62

social mobilisation. The state is the major employer, and has undertaken ambitious economic, educational and social development projects that have extended its power to all sections of society. Its capabilities to engage in social mobilisation have been greatly aided by the state's extractive powers, which have enabled it to use Iraq's massive oil wealth to finance the growth of state activities and state power. This wealth has also enabled the state to expand its capacity for institutionalised violence. A huge army has been built up, and party rule has been enforced by a large and ever-present internal security apparatus. Attempts by the state to control the population have also relied heavily on the use of symbolism for political mobilisation through the state-controlled and state-nurtured mass media. In its symbolism, the state has highlighted nationalistic themes designed to provide citizens with a sense of common identity that could help to unify the country against real or alleged threats from other Middle Eastern countries.

The Iraqi state possesses many characteristics that are hypothesised by the political theories discussed earlier to be associated with a propensity for external conflict. Iraq is a dictatorship, in which there is no free public discussion of foreign policy, and no public input into or constraints on decisions on the making of war and peace. Moreover, problems of internal heterogeneity and sectarian and ethnic cleavages have made the maintenance of territorial integrity a primary concern of the state, to be accomplished by means varying from the threat or use of force to crush externally-supported rebellions, to the political mobilisation of the population around the fear of foreign threats.

A number of the problems facing the state arise directly from its origins in the post-First World War settlement of the borders of the Middle East by the colonial powers. In the drawing of the map of what would eventually become the new nation-state system in the Middle East, Britain and France were careful not to endow any of the new states with characteristics that would allow it to become too powerful. Iraq was allocated borders that meant that it was essentially landlocked and surrounded by six countries with differing interests. Its ethnic and sectarian composition cut across regional borders in ways likely to pose problems between the state of Iraq and its Iranian neighbour.

Iraq's first foreign war under the leadership of Saddam Hussein was against Iran, and it set the stage for the second, against Kuwait. Although, in 1975 Saddam had resolved one major source of conflict with the Shah of Iran, an Iranian-backed Kurdish rebellion, tension with Iran flared up again after the Iranian revolution in 1979. When the regime of the Ayatollah Khomeini began to voice strong commitments to revolutionary Islamic evangelism, Iraq feared that it would be a prime target of Iranian attempts to promote Shi'a fundamentalism, especially since the majority of its own population was Shi'a. At the same time, as the Iranian revolution progressed, Iraq also saw an opportunity to obtain a regional advantage through war – one that would allow it to exploit the military weakness caused by Iran's revolutionary turmoil, and remedy the geo-strategic weaknesses imposed on Iraq at the time of its creation by the colonial powers.

The tremendous economic and human losses brought about by the war with Iran from 1980–88 made it extremely difficult for the Iraqi government to retain the always precarious allegiance of its various ethnic minorities. No sooner had the war with Iran ended and a cease-fire agreement been signed than the political strength and social unity of Iraq as a nation state began to falter. Many families had lost loved ones in the war. After these profound sacrifices of life and limb, with the coming of peace the Iraqi nation saw a decline in its basic standard of living rather than the prosperity it and the Iraqi government had awaited. Domestic turmoil seemed certain.

Aware of the discontent of the people, the government mounted a two-pronged campaign: first, it sought to revive Iraqi nationalism through propaganda emphasising legendary Arab glories and achievements; second, it proffered various measures to alleviate the economic plight of the Iraqi people. Chief among these were a liberalisation of the economy and a broadening of the base of popular political participation. When this two-pronged approach failed, the government finally resorted to the invasion of Kuwait in an attempt to resolve its problems. Kuwait represented an economic prize sufficient to solve all the financial ills which had befallen Iraq. Kuwait was also unpopular among ordinary Iraqis because of its enormous wealth. Kuwaiti policies on the repayment by Iraq of debts incurred during the war, and on issues of oil pricing, were viewed by Iraq as hostile. The humiliation of Kuwait would, it was believed, do much to reinvigorate Iraqi nationalist sentiments and restore Iraqi national pride.

It was against this complex interplay of factors that the invasion of Kuwait occurred. In order to fully understand the motives that prompted the invasion from the perspective of the Iraqi state, it is helpful to examine the varied and often competing political and social forces that operated within the country. To this end, it will be necessary first to outline the creation and nature of the Iraqi state with particular reference to its ethnic make-up and the political instability that this produced, with resulting pressure on the state to enforce internal cohesion. The importance of one particular and unique ethnic minority, the Kurds, will be discussed in some detail.

The most important organ of the polity in Iraq is the Ba'th party which runs the state and enjoys virtual monopoly control of the state forces. The Ba'th party is predominantly composed of Sunni Muslims, and this was a principal reason why the Shi'a Muslim revolution in Iran was considered to be a major threat to the state of Iraq. The war waged against Iran in 1980–88 was a turning point for Iraq. Had the eight-year war been averted, together with all its incalculable consequences for Iraq, then Iraq would never have been in a situation where its leadership saw the invasion of Kuwait as its best option. The Iran–Iraq war, therefore, will be considered as a springboard, the power of which eventually caused Iraq to propel its forces into Kuwait. Finally, the war with Kuwait will briefly be considered.

The Creation of the State of Iraq

The state of Iraq as it is known today has only existed since 1921, when its borders were artificially created out of three provinces of the former Ottoman empire at a meeting in Cairo. It was entrusted to Britain and known as the Kingdom of Iraq. The new state included the cities of Baghdad, Basra and Mosul. Its borders, however, also incorporated diverse sectarian groups, the most important of which were the Sunnis, and the Shi'a and an important non-Arab national minority, the Kurds. Other, smaller minorities also existed within the new state, among them Persians, Christians, Turks, and Jews.

The British, as evidence of their preponderant influence, provided Iraq with a king who was not of Iraqi origin: Feisal, the son of the Sherif of Mecca. 'You may rely on one thing,' one participant later wrote back to London. 'I'll never engage in creating Kings again ... It is too great a strain.'[1] The task of ruling so many diverse elements within artificial borders, which reflected foreign interests rather than local reality, was soon found by the king to be a daunting one. In a confidential memorandum, King Feisal wrote:

> there is still – and I say this with a heart full of sorrow – no Iraqi people but unimaginable masses of human beings, devoid of any patriotic idea, imbued with religious traditions and absurdities, connected by no common tie, giving ear to evil, prone to anarchy, and perpetually ready to rise against any government whatever. Out of these masses we want to fashion a people which we would train, educate and refine ... The circumstances, being what they are, the immenseness of the efforts needed for this [can be imagined].[2]

Despite the many, often antagonistic sects that divided Iraq as it was created, its boundaries did in fact follow a natural geographical region. Mesopotamia (in Greek, the land between two rivers) was once the name given to identify the area surrounded by the Tigris and Euphrates rivers, the home of the Sumerians and of the biblical Old Testament patriarch Abraham. The same region was called al-Rafadin in Arabic, a name still used in Iraq today, which means 'the land of the two rivers'.[3] The region was prominent in ancient history. It was the centre of the Babylonian empire, led by the great statesman and early lawgiver, Hammurabi, under whose reign Babylonia thrived and prospered. The prestige of Babylon was further enhanced under Nebuchadnezzar, who extended its empire to include Jerusalem, destroying its temple when he conquered the city in 507 BC.

The legendary ancient heritage of Iraq has often been invoked in speeches by Saddam Hussein as a theme of contemporary political mobilisation. The culture of Mesopotamia, as seen in the historical achievements of the civilisations of Sumer, Akkad, and Babylon, has been exalted by Iraqi leaders for propaganda purposes, both domestically and abroad.[4] Museum openings, archaeological digs, and theatrical offerings all remind Iraqis of their ties to their cultural predecessors, as part of an attempt by the government to ensure that Iraq's ancient cultural heritage remains alive and vibrant in the minds and hearts of its people.

Part of Iraq's legacy is a geographical position that placed it squarely in the cross-roads of marauding invaders. Since the sixteenth century ended, modern-day Iraq has been plagued by foreign invaders, eager to seize the bounty of an area blessed by God. This history of foreign intervention and domination has influenced the behaviour of today's Iraqi leaders and shaped their political outlook. President Saddam Hussein wastes no opportunity to remind the people that 'Turkey once imposed on us the Turkish language and culture ... They used to take turns [to humiliate] Iraq. Turkey goes and Iran comes. All this under the guise of Islam. Enough ... We are Iraqis and are part of the Arab homeland and the Arab nation. Iraq belongs to us.'[5] In this way, although the people of Iraq are divided by religious, ethnic or political beliefs, they are urged to find in their glorious past a common ground for unity based on mutual interests.

Other powerful factors exerting an influence over Iraq's foreign policy stem from the establishment by the colonial powers after the First World War of the framework for the Middle Eastern nation-state system. Primary among them is the British imposition of borders making Iraq virtually landlocked, and surrounded by six countries, none of which is a natural ally. Two of these, Turkey and Iran, are non-Arab, and are also more populous and more powerful. Syria has been an arch-rival and a formidable foe, especially in the Arab political realm. Saudi Arabia, Kuwait, and Jordan, while not at all equal to Iraq in terms of power or population, have generally been neither sympathetic nor antagonistic. In the case of Kuwait, there has been a major territorial dispute, since Iraq has frequently claimed that Kuwait was historically part of Iraq.

The harsh fact and underlying reality is that Iraq's borders leave it extremely exposed and vulnerable.[6] At the same time, it is endowed with an abundance of desirable natural resources, including oil, as well as fertile agricultural lands. It therefore faces several interrelated burdens to maintain its own territorial integrity – diplomacy, military vigilance on its borders, and the financial cost of that vigilance.

In addition to its exposed geopolitical position, Iraq also has a problem with water. Before the bonanza of the oil price explosions of the 1970s, the Tigris and Euphrates rivers were its two most important sources of revenue. Not only were they important for agriculture, but they also provided essential hydroelectric power for a nation coming into its own.[7] Even today, despite the diminishing role of agriculture, the rivers remain the country's primary source of fresh water. Iraq's dependence on them only exacerbates its vulnerability since control of the source and of the flow of each river lies in unfriendly or, at least, undependable hands.

Both rivers rise in the mountains of Turkey; the Tigris enters Iraqi territory directly from there, but the Euphrates passes first through Syria. Thus, Iraq is in effect a hostage to the political mood and will of its two neighbours, neither of which can be considered a reliable economic partner or political ally. Neither so far has taken advantage of this situation. On the other hand, both have been willing to cut off Iraqi oil passing through their territories, even when the action has meant considerable economic loss to them.

Iraq's lack of access to international waters is a political and economic drawback of immense proportions which is perceived by its leaders and by ordinary Iraqis as a persistent danger to their daily survival. This consideration, more than any other, enabled Saddam Hussein to lead his country into two devastating wars. During the invasions both of Iran and later of Kuwait the leadership commanded – at least initially – respectable general support among the people.

The most serious and enduring dilemma confronting Iraq, however, is its diverse ethnic and religious make-up. The boundaries of modern Iraq were drawn with less regard for demographic realities than for narrow European political and economic interests. This resulted in the establishment of a unique, and at root mutually antipathetic amalgam of cultures, beliefs, and races. An understanding of this amalgam, and the resulting social tensions, is essential to any examination of foreign or domestic Iraqi political policies.

There are two basic cleavages within the Iraqi population: religious and ethnic. The religious division lies between the Shi'a Muslim majority, approximately 60 per cent of the population, and the Sunni Muslim minority, constituting less than 30 per cent of the population, who nevertheless dominate the government. The ethnic division is one which separates Arabs and the non-Arab Kurds. The situation is further complicated by the fact that the Kurds are Sunni Muslims who have over the years established themselves as a powerful force within Iraq. The Kurds have posed the principal ethnic-political challenge to Iraq in its recent history. The Kurdish problem has affected both the domestic policy of the government of Iraq, and the foreign policy of the state, since the Kurdish problem affects Iraqi relations with neighbours, especially Iran, which have Kurdish populations. The history and political identity of the Kurds thus demands special attention.

The Kurds

Scattered today over five countries, Iran, Turkey, Iraq, Syria and parts of the former Soviet Union, the Kurds have been dominated throughout their history by the many empires that have ruled the area. Their population today is estimated at between 8 and 18 million – depending on the bias of the writer.

In the aftermath of the First World War Britain reneged on an agreement with the Kurds to accord them full independence, preferring to establish a more stable Iraq which would include the oil-rich (and predominantly Kurdish) north. In return, the Iraqi government promised to grant the Kurds 'internationally recognised status of a kind never conceded to the Kurds of Turkey and Iran'.[8] In the event these Iraqi political guarantees were never fulfilled. In frustration the Kurds have resorted to acts of hostility and violence, usually of a fairly minor nature.

It was not until 1968, when the Ba'th party seized power, that the political question of the Kurds attained any prominence. The Kurdish Democratic Party (KDP)'s political influence as a pressure group had been growing steadily before then. Since the KDP was a specifically non-Arab political party diametrically opposed to the Ba'th party's long-held tenets of Arab nationalism and Arab unity, a clash was inevitable. The first major disagreement between the two parties occurred when the union of Iraq with Egypt (the United Arab Republic, or UAR) was proposed. Ba'th support for this move was received with a singular lack of enthusiasm by the KDP.[9] Yet the Ba'th party, still endeavouring to consolidate its political position, could ill afford a political confrontation with a contender for power, and backed away from a unity with Egypt. Led by Saddam Hussein, the Iraqi government adopted a pragmatic approach towards the Kurds; in 1970 the regime reached an agreement with Kurdish nationalists which recognised, among other things, the Kurdish right to autonomous rule.[10]

In the years that followed, Iraq's internal political and economic balance of power changed in favour of the ruling Ba'th party. Oil prices started their meteoric rise. Since Iraq already had nationalised its oil industry, the resulting financial bonanza secured and enhanced the regime's stability. Iraq's dispute with its powerful neighbour Iran, a traditional ally of the Kurds against Iraq, headed towards political mediation. With the absence of any urgent need to appease the Kurds, relations began to deteriorate between them and the Iraqi government. A Kurdish resistance movement began to gather strength. In a calculated move aimed at eliminating any serious Kurdish opposition, a full year before the Iraqi government signed the 1975 Algiers treaty with the Shah of Iran, the Iraqi army launched a ruthless offensive against the Kurdish resistance movement, and virtually crushed it.

By the time of the 1979 revolution in Iran, with the Shah's fall from power and Ayatollah Khomeini's ascendance, conflict between the Kurds and the Iraqi government had recommenced. Iranian support of the Kurds had led to the formation of the more powerful Iraq Kurdistan Front (IKF), jointly led by Jalal Talabani and Massoud Barzani.[11] Although the leadership of the Kurds was fluid and complex, the IKF was the most serious internal threat the Ba'th party had to confront.

The possibility of Kurdish secession remained real and terrifying to the ruling elite in Baghdad. The Kurds not only inhabited and dominated the prized oil-rich northern region of Iraq, al-Mosul, but their presence and strength there raised the real threat of their attaining full independence. This development would have had a potential domino effect, effectively ending any hopes of Arab unity, of which Iraq had always cast itself in the role of champion. In its efforts to avoid this worst-case scenario, the Iraqi Ba'th party embarked on a carrot-and-stick policy, making few actual concessions but appeasing the Kurdish leadership through costly distributions of wealth in the form of regional economic development or direct cash payments. Its other option would have been to order extensive and coercive military measures which, in addition to being equally costly, would have diverted the government's attention from other important issues.

The significance of the Kurdish issue was not confined to Iraq's internal affairs. It played a central role in foreign policy *vis-à-vis* Khomeini's Iran. Both countries had major ethnic Kurd populations within their territory, and both attempted to mollify or suppress those Kurds within their own borders while simultaneously trying to incite the Kurds next door to insurrection. When the Kurdish leader Talabani was criticised for shifting towards improved relations with Saddam, he replied, 'At least we can talk to Saddam Hussein ... Khomeini has killed 20,000 Iranian Kurds and sees all minorities as agents of Satan.'[12] Although there were growing numbers of Kurdish (and Shi'a) representatives in the Iraqi parliament, their participation remained symbolic.

The challenge to the Baghdad government represented by Iraqi Kurds was one which highlighted the difficulties posed to states by ethnic or other minorities whose population concentrations extend across state borders. Not only are these minorities seen by states as possible threats to territorial integrity, which may need to be suppressed by force; they also offer a temptation for states to weaken rival states by attempting to manipulate their ethnic minorities. In addition to the Kurds, Iran had an Arab minority concentrated in its main oil-producing region. In the war with Iran, Iraq clearly had high expectations for support from these ethnic Arabs in Iran; but no such support materialised. Conversely, Iran hoped for support from the Shi'a community in Iraq during the Iran–Iraq war, but this expectation also proved unfounded. When domestic and foreign problems are closely related, so that a state's perceived domestic threats become major concerns of foreign policy, there is clearly a strong possibility that domestic pressures will engender a belligerent foreign policy.

The Ba'th Party

The Ba'th party (in English, the Party of the Arab Renaissance or Reawakening) held its first congress in Damascus in 1947, at which it reinforced the commitment of its members to the ultimate political unification of the entire Arab world.[13] The party was founded by Salah al-Din al-Bitar, a Muslim, and Michel Aflaq, a Christian, both of whom came from modest backgrounds and were educated at the Sorbonne in Paris. Its adherents saw the party primarily as an expression of Arab nationalism, and the one body capable of achieving the Arab secular dream of political unification.[14] Its appeal was broad and, with its idealistic tenets, it found supporters in many Arab countries, including Iraq.

Once the Iraqi Ba'th party was established in Baghdad and had gathered strength in the country and in the army, it succeeded in gaining power through a military coup in 1963, after which 'the crucial threads of government became almost entirely centred in its hands.'[15] Although there were challenges to its power, and the party made a series of political miscalculations which resulted in its ouster from government for four years, it learned from its mistakes and regained its foothold in 1968 in a military coup. Eventually it achieved a ruthless domination of all the major centres of the government and the army. In this way Iraq – which had experienced more violent domestic turmoil than most countries in the Middle East – became stable (if by decidedly draconian means).

The first steps in the consolidation of the party's power began with purges in the top echelons of the party apparatus and the military. Any officials or officers of questionable loyalty were either replaced, forced to retire or put on trial for offences against the state, usually with fatal consequences. New members were recruited to conduct clandestine party operations. Tariq Aziz, a Christian, and a prominent member of the Ba'th, once remarked that 'the Arab Ba'th Socialist Party [ABSP] is not a conventional political organisation, but is composed of cells of valiant revolutionaries ... They are experts in secret organisation. They are organisers of demonstrations, strikes, and armed revolutions ... They [are] the knights of struggle.'[16] As Kamel Abu Jaber explains, the Ba'th party's 'pyramidal structure begins with the Halaqah (Cell) at the bottom and the National Command and the Secretary General at the top... [similar to Communist or Fascist parties who] alone have the cell as their basis'.[17]

In Iraq, the nation-wide process of Ba'thisation increased the number of its members to almost 10 per cent of the total population.[18] Although less than 1 per cent of these were in fact full party members, Saddam Hussein once compared the Ba'th party to a ship, saying that 'with God's help not one person will be left outside this ship ... This ship is so big that it encompasses the whole of Iraq.'[19] Such claims reflect the Iraqi leadership's strategy of creating a united ideological front as a means of pre-empting internal political dissent. 'With our party methods, there is no chance for anyone who disagrees with us to jump on a couple of tanks and overthrow the government.'[20] Saddam Hussein recognised the brutal necessity of his party's autocratic methods as a part of its historical progression: 'We are now in our Stalinist era. We shall strike with an iron fist against the slightest deviation or backsliding, beginning with the Ba'this themselves.'[21]

As with the Communist Party of the former Soviet Union, where one grouping, the ethnic Russians, dominated the Politburo, in Iraq Sunni Muslims accounted for 84.9 per cent of the top command of the party, while Shi'a members represented only 5.7 per cent.[22] But the Ba'th party differed from the communist Politburo in one notable way: it was increasingly dominated by one tribal family, the Takritis. The pervasive presence of these Sunni Takritis was seen particularly in their control of the important security and defence-related portfolios at the ministerial level. The mastery exercised by the Takritis over the Ba'th party was so blatant that the most authoritative scholar on modern Iraq, Hanna Batatu, was prompted to note that 'it would not be going too far to say that the Takritis rule through the Ba'th party, rather than that the Ba'th party rule through the Takritis.'[23]

Iraq under the Ba'th faced a problem identified as long ago as 1947 by the noted scholar and analyst Albert Hourani: the country could not become united internally or achieve a stable political structure until two fundamental issues had been faced and resolved: the Sunni–Shi'a relationship and Iraq's relationship with the Arab world.[24] Yet, the Ba'th party in Iraq, with its deep divisions and its disregard for the interests of important ethnic groups, itself incorporated the central dilemma facing Iraq: the lack of a common identity to which the whole nation subscribed. As a representative of the Sunni Muslim minority, the Ba'th party has faced the temptation of toning down the long-held party line calling for national unity. A dilution of the theme of unity would, however, run the risk of undermining the monopoly control of the Ba'th, since slogans urging unity and solidarity can be used to attempt to cover social rifts arising from regional and economic discrimination.

The Ba'th party's predicament has been further complicated by its oscillation between two competing ideologies: Iraqism and Arabism. The Kurds, for example, make it abundantly clear that while they are Sunni Muslims, they are not Arabs, and therefore they oppose all Ba'th party talk of Arab nationalism. Understandably, they are not willing to relinquish their Kurdish national identity for the sake of Arab nationalism. Therefore, Ba'th elites in Baghdad have been confronted by a major problem of identity:

> The Ba'th dilemma over the question of identity is reflected in its approach to the two competing 'nationalisms' – Iraqi nationalism versus Arab nationalism, or *wataniyya Iraqiyya* versus *qawmiyya Arabiyya*. Since Iraq's inception these two trends have been vying for ascendancy: while the first preached loyalty to the Iraqi state and sought to develop its particularism and 'unity within,' the second preached

loyalty to the Arab nation, placing emphasis on 'unity without' and
on the whole rather than on a single country.[25]

By the time of the invasion of Iran, the rhetoric of Pan-Arab unity had
been put aside by Iraq in order to pursue better relations with the Arab
Gulf countries, including Kuwait and Saudi Arabia. Saddam Hussein
reflected that new reality on 8 September 1980, just before the war
with Iran, in a statement demonstrating a considerable modification of
the pan-Arab viewpoint:

> The Iraqis are now of the opinion that Arab unity can only take
> place after a clear demarcation of borders between all countries. We
> further believe that Arab unity must not take place through the
> elimination of the local and national characteristics of any Arab
> country. If the people in the PDRY [the former south Yemen]... wish
> to establish unity with Iraq today on the basis of dissolving the Iraqi
> and Yemeni personalities, I, Saddam Hussein, will personally object
> to such unity. I will say: Let the two personalities coexist with one
> another.
>
> The question of linking unity to the removal of boundaries is no
> longer acceptable to present Arab mentality. It could have been
> acceptable ten or twenty years ago ... Any Arab would have wished
> to see the Arab nation as one state ... But these are sheer dreams.
> The Arab reality is that the Arabs are now 22 states, and we have to
> behave accordingly. Therefore, unity must not be imposed, but must
> be achieved through common fraternal opinion. Unity must give
> strength to its partners, not cancel their national identity.[26]

Although other important institutions are part of the Iraqi government
– including the once powerful Revolutionary Command Council (RCC),
the National Assembly (NA), and the military – over the years they
have all become totally subservient to the Ba'th party, and thus to
Saddam Hussein. Powerful members of the RCC, for example, were
ousted when their loyalty to Saddam became suspect. The NA, created
by Hussein in 1989, was nothing more than a rubber stamp for his
political wishes, as was demonstrated during the invasion of Kuwait
when it not only endorsed all his plans but applauded him personally.
And although Iraq's military has emerged as one of the largest and
most powerful forces in the Middle East, its officers have been subject
to constant surveillance; in particular, they have been selected more for

THE STATE OF IRAQ

their loyalty than for their competence, although their military power has nevertheless been well-respected.

The state's control and power are seen in the three overlapping components of the Iraqi system – the Ba'th party organisation, the government bureaucracy, and the military and security forces. It is the input of the 'system' rather than that of the citizens which establishes and delineates the government's political capacity.[27] In other words, the citizens' demands (i.e. for political participation) go unheeded by the government, while Iraqi society nevertheless continues to play its part in supporting the government (i.e. by obeying the law and offering no serious opposition to public authority).

If one determinant more than any other has enabled the state of Iraq to maintain its strength and thus its political stability, it is income derived from oil rents, which has enhanced the state's capacity on almost all fronts. Revenues at the state's disposal from oil increased from $487 million in 1968 when the Ba'th took power, to $6.7 billion in 1974 and to $12.2 billion in 1979, shortly before the attack on Iran.[28]

After the Ba'th party came to power in 1968, the government greatly expanded its control of the economy: at the time of the Gulf War government organisations accounted for 78 per cent of GNP and purchased 90 per cent of imported goods. Oil (which is entirely owned by the government) contributed almost 60 per cent of the GNP and constituted almost 98 per cent of all exports.[29] The government, furthermore, owns and operates all the country's heavy industries. Iraq's oil-based economy, with its highly centralised institutions, has enabled the state to control the economy from the top, thus affecting every individual on the bottom by its control of resource allocation.

While Iraq has been able to draw on sufficient support to rule through the 'system input,' and has failed to meet the demand side, it is in the conversion function of the 'system output' that the state's capability has been most visible. The state's extractive capability is particularly significant, since it does not have to extract taxes from its citizens. Instead, it raises revenues through oil rent, without political cost to the government. Indeed, this system of obtaining revenues tends to instil or deepen popular allegiance and support to the government.

Because of the Iraqi state's easy access to huge revenues, the regime has confidently embarked upon costly policies of intervention and control, designed to maximise the economic leverage needed to ensure

popular acquiescence and political support.[30] Economic control has gone
hand-in-hand with political control, resulting in a regulative state, with
strong capabilities and control over everything from the individual's
right to religious belief to basic questions of his economic and political
freedom.

It is because of Iraq's unique ability to raise its revenues without
taxing its people that the state's capacity for distribution is so high.
Adnan Hamadani, head of Iraqi economic planning, has noted: 'The
Ba'th party is not just a ruling party; it has an ideology based on rapid
development of the economy in a limited period of time. For this we
need large revenues.'[31]

Nowhere is the intricate relationship between state and society more
visible than in the government's employment programmes. By 1977 the
state was by far the largest employer in Iraq. Joe Stork provides an
authoritative description of Iraq's employment policy:

> [Government service] is now the largest sector in terms of employ-
> ment: over one million people in 1977. Much of the labour displaced
> from the agricultural sector in recent years has been absorbed in this
> sector, and most of it by the state itself. The state is by far the largest
> single employer. In 1977 the number of government personnel was
> 580,132, almost as many people as employed by all large public and
> private manufacturing firms combined. This does not include the
> armed forces, an estimated 230,000, or nearly 200,000 pensioners
> directly dependent on the state for their livelihood. Within the govern-
> ment the largest employer is the Ministry of the Interior, with 136,900
> in 1977. Another 40,819 were employed in the Presidential Affairs
> Department, many of whom, as in the Interior Ministry, were engaged
> in 'security' assignments. In November 1979 [after Saddam became
> president], Interior Minister Shakur announced an unspecified expan-
> sion of internal security forces 'in order to carry out transactions with
> citizens with the greatest possible speed.'[32]

All of this reveals both the capacity of the Iraqi state and the extremes
to which it is willing to go in order to ensure its monopoly of power
and to continue popular dependency on the regime. Given that the
cost of maintaining the security forces must be a considerable burden
on state revenues, the distributive state capability in Iraq scores high
compared to other Middle Eastern countries. Supported by the second
highest oil reserves in the Middle East, after those of Saudi Arabia,

Iraq's high levels of oil production have been able to finance major government expenditures on education, health care, social welfare programmes and various community projects. Indeed, the social welfare system has guaranteed many benefits that usually only liberal countries with high standards of living can afford.

The symbolic capability of the state of Iraq is also unsurpassed in the region – save perhaps by Syria's Ba'th party and the Islamic Republic of Iran. The Iraqi Ba'th has ruled effectively for many years behind an effective facade of rhetoric and crude political symbolism. A diet of political rhetoric about the Ba'th revolution is fed to children beginning in their early years in school. A wholesale, pervasive, and skilful indoctrination in the state's ideology has been a factor in the Ba'thisation of large numbers of citizens. The invasions of Iran and Kuwait were both preceded by an onslaught of government propaganda employing sophisticated symbolism designed to gather support behind the government. While there is no reliable way of gauging the level of popular Iraqi support for the war in a state without popular participation, the fact that there was no political coup d'état or military mutiny may be indicative of a fairly high general level of approval, or at least acceptance of government propaganda.

Statues and portraits of Saddam Hussein are omnipresent in today's Iraq. Teenagers in Iraq have known no other important national political figure. More than simply representing the state, he *is* the state. On a similarly symbolic level, too, the war with Iran was mythologised by being dubbed 'Qadisiyya,' referring to a battle in the Arab–Persian war in the early Islamic period, which the Arabs won decisively.

The creation of an effective symbolic state capability has paid off handsomely for Saddam Hussein in political terms. Not only has it reinforced the government's regulative capability, but it has ensured widespread acceptance of the state and its political agenda under the banner of its well-marketed ideology.

In its handling of the state's responsive capability, however, the ruling Ba'th party has failed dismally. By any measure, state responsiveness rates very low indeed. While the official manifesto of the Ba'th party promises freedom, this is only to be granted after Arab unity and true socialism have been achieved. Even so, the party seems to have judged correctly just what it can get away with in terms of the imbalance between the state's capability for input and output.

The state capability in Iraq and its willingness to respond to its citizens' needs is, at least in theory, greater than that of some of its neighbours. Kuwait and Bahrain, for example, both suspended their parliaments altogether, in 1986 and 1976 respectively. In Iraq under Saddam, on the other hand, even during the purge years of his climb to power, the National Assembly continued to function, although with very little real authority. It has served his purposes very well. First, it reinforces his notion of himself as a leader ruling with unreserved popular support. Secondly, it acts as his watchdog, legitimately keeping an eye on government officials and – if less legitimately – removing and/or indicting those of whom Hussein does not approve.[33]

Even while the war was raging with Iran, Saddam put forward an agenda for political reform, economic liberalisation and freedom of the press. This programme was in addition to the popular (if largely cosmetic) measure he had already enacted, opening a direct line between himself and the common people, enabling them to air their grievances to the highest authority in the land. Another politically astute move by the Iraqi leader (often reported in the Arab press and carried live on Iraqi television) has been his habit of visiting the suburbs of Baghdad incognito, supposedly to ascertain at first hand the needs of 'his' people. More than any other government in the region, Baghdad has understood the power of television – so much so that, in order to maximise the effectiveness of its state-run service, the government has distributed television sets free of charge.

The government has also understood that certain segments of society require a higher level of responsiveness. As part of its carrot-and-stick policy, therefore, even at times when it was actively trying to suppress the Shi'a and Kurdish communities, the Ba'th party embarked on beneficial economic projects in their areas, which included the construction of places of religious worship. More importantly, the army's support was guaranteed by large salary increases and a boost for the military industry.[34]

Any impartial evaluation of the Iraqi state's output capability must point out its many positive aspects. One important achievement has been the creation of national cohesion within the state of Iraq, despite the challenge of its unique mixture of ethnic and religious groups. During Iraq's war with the Shi'a regime of Iran, the co-operation of the Iraqi Shi'a with the government was not gained by repressive measures: clearly they chose to see themselves as Arab-Iraqis rather than in terms of their religious affiliation.[35] Although the same cannot be said of the Kurds, this Iraqi achievement of building domestic communal solidarity is one few neighbouring countries could match.

Inevitably, the state's growing domestic prowess meant that its regional stature heightened, too. In the course of establishing its control domestically, however, it experienced pressures to look outward and adopt a belligerent foreign policy as a means of consolidating its rule or attempting to resolve domestic crises. Thus, the Iraqi state invaded two of its neighbours within one decade, Iran in 1980 and Kuwait in 1990.

The Iraq–Iran War

The war with Iran between 1980 and 1988 was important on a number of counts. Iraq ascended to a more important status in the region, thanks to its claimed 'victory' over Iran. The 'Arab victory' over a traditional enemy also added to the regime's lustre and provided an important additional psychological boost for the leadership. Furthermore, the conduct of the war obliged Iraq, almost without any notice, to acquire a military capability that was unquestionably the greatest in the Arab world.

The modern history of border conflicts and territorial disputes between Iran and Iraq can be traced back to the rivalries which existed between the Ottoman empire and the Persian empire 400 years ago.[36] The area has in fact been so contentious that there have been at least five major, well-known attempts to bring peace there, beginning with the treaty of 1639 and ending with the Constantinople Protocol of 1913.[37] The most recent agreement was concluded in Algeria in 1975 between the Shah of Iran and the then vice-president of Iraq, Saddam Hussein. It was an abrogation of this agreement that provided the pretext for Iraq's war with Iran in September 1980.

Curiously, despite the traditional animosities of the region, the regimes of Iraq and Iran share many features. Both have Shi'a majority populations, both are beset with minority Kurdish rebels, both are driven by rigid ideologies, and both claim to be revolutionary. And both Iraq's Ba'th party and the Islamic Republic of Iran have at one time or another expressed their commitment to exporting their ideologies to neighbouring states. None of these similarities has lessened historical animosities.

If proof were needed of the antipathy between these two traditional enemies, it is found in the merciless conduct of the war of attrition, which claimed as many as 1.7 million lives, including civilian casualties, from the populations of the two foes.[38] The hostility goes well beyond territorial ambitions. Conflicting ideologies, personalities and hopes for regional power were major additional motivating forces behind the war and its purposeless continuation. A broad summary of background events leading to the war is useful here.

An appropriate point of departure is the 1975 accord between the two countries. At that time Iran was striving openly to become the most powerful country in the Gulf and, under US patronage, the policeman of the area. It might be thought surprising, therefore, that Iraq, under the influence of its politically ambitious rising star, Saddam Hussein, should have acceded to the shah's demands and signed the accord, especially since both leaders regarded each other with deep disdain. But the agreement provided desperately needed gains for each side. Iran agreed to close its borders to the Kurds, thus effectively ending that damaging revolt and challenge to Iraqi rule, while Iraq, in return, agreed to surrender its claim to sovereignty over the entire Shatt al-Arab.[39] The Shatt al-Arab waterway, a river formed by the confluence of the Tigris and the Euphrates, would play an important role in shaping future relations between the two countries. Moreover, its significance to Iraq was (and is) crucial, for it provides its only link with the sea. Since Iran's concession concerning the Kurds was, by comparison, only minor, for the land-locked Iraq to give up its right to access to the waterway to the sea constituted *de facto* recognition of the shah's superiority at that time. It also marked Saddam's low point as a political player in the region.

After the agreement, the Gulf area remained stable for a while. But with the coming of the Iranian revolution in 1979, the situation changed. Miron Rezun explains:

> Having become the undisputed leader of Iraq in 1979, the Iraqi president carefully took time out to observe what the Ayatollah Khomeini was up to when the Iranian ecclesiastic also consolidated his power in the same year. Saddam must have watched with particular glee as the Shah went to defeat and went off to an undignified exile and premature death. He watched and waited as the Iranian army was being pilloried by the Islamic Revolution and then indiscriminately

purged of its best officers and pilots while radical religious leaders came to power. He must have reacted with horror, too, as he realised the potential of the new fundamentalism that was sweeping across the entire Middle East. Radical fundamentalism could easily cost him his own power inside Iraq. The Shi'a Muslims were, after all, in a slight majority in Iraq. No sooner was Khomeini sitting snugly in power than he made it known how much he hoped that Iraq would also become an Islamic republic.[40]

One of the first serious indications of Iran's ill intentions towards its neighbours came in Khomeini's 1979 declaration:

> We will export our revolution throughout the world because it is an Islamic revolution. The struggle will continue until the calls 'there is no god but God' and 'Mohammed is the messenger of God' are echoed all over the world. The struggle will continue as long as the oppressors subjugate people in every corner of the world.[41]

The Islamic republic soon extended its political rhetoric to include attacks upon Iraq and its leadership, a development which Iraq considered a deliberate provocation. Khomeini, who himself had lived in Iraq in 1965 and later was abandoned by Iraq after its deal with the Shah of Iran, denounced the Ba'th as secular and racist, and accused it of discriminating among believers on the basis of their national and/ or ethno-cultural identities.[42] The Islamic Republic also overtly incited revolution among Iraq's Shi'a population: among the results of this campaign was an attempt on the life of a senior Ba'th official, Tariq Aziz, by a Shi'a of Iraqi origin in April 1980.[43]

Iraq's response to these challenges was a full military invasion of Iran on 17 September 1980. In a provocative and uncompromising speech reminiscent of the dramatic rhetoric of the late Gamal Abdul Nasser, Saddam announced before the Iraqi National Assembly his decision to abrogate the 1975 agreement.

The war with Iran was very costly. Even more importantly, however, it can now be seen to have been waged without any clear political or military objectives. Furthermore, as Shahram Chubin, a noted expert in the politics of the area points out, it was waged inexpertly.

> Iraq's inability to capitalise on surprise in the early weeks of the war to military effect was not as serious as its failure to fashion a clear political objective. It seems to have expected either a quick collapse

of the regime, or a willingness to sue for peace, based on limited
losses. This completely misjudged the nature of revolutionary systems
which do not traditionally understand or wage limited wars (let alone
a revolution based on the Shi'i emphasis on the positive value of
martyrdom and sacrifice).[44]

It is probable, in fact, that Iraq's invasion, by providing an external
enemy against whom Iran's various warring internal factions could
unite, was precisely what the precarious revolution in Tehran needed to
prolong its survival. In contrast to the economically vibrant Iraq, Iran
faced economic difficulties. The international community was apprehensive about extending co-operation to its extremist regime, and its oil
production had been dramatically reduced. In addition, Iran's once
powerful military was beset by uncertainties. Accused of sympathising
with the late shah, its top leadership were either executed or ran for
cover. Additionally, Iran's traditional military suppliers, mainly the USA
and Western European countries, were no longer prepared to co-operate
– especially after the 1979 American hostage seizure.

Such developments obviously influenced the Iraqi leadership in the
months prior to the invasion of Iran. The expectation of a quick victory,
however, was not realised in the reality of the battlefields. The conflict
stalled through poor generalship on both sides, becoming in effect an
eight-year war of attrition, distinguished by the launching of long-range
missiles against civilians and the use of weapons of mass destruction,
including gas. By 1988, both combatants were on their knees. Khomeini
had likened any acceptance of a cease-fire with Iraq to taking poison,
but nonetheless, he eventually swallowed it.

Military might is notoriously expensive. While the war with Iran
elevated Iraq's status in the Middle East, along with its aspirations to
Arab leadership, it also left Iraq financially crippled. The Iraqi leadership quickly discovered how difficult it was to run a country no longer
on a war footing and no longer united in common cause against a
common enemy. Among the important problems that now confronted
the Iraqi leadership were high military expenditure, low oil production
and low prices, a faltering domestic economy, and a growing international debt. All of these matters required immediate attention, and
there was little room for error.

Having heralded the end of the war as a great victory, the Ba'th
leadership quickly found itself hostage to its own promises. Throughout

the conflict, the expectations of the people had been inflated by assurances of the prosperity that would come once the war was won. Now that the war had indeed finally ended, the least the people expected was that the army would be demobilised so that ordinary family and village life could be resumed.

Faced with popular discontent, and aware of their regime's lack of political legitimacy, Iraqi leaders understood that resorting to traditional methods and unleashing the internal security force would not be sufficient to defuse the situation. Instead, as Freedman and Karsh point out, they tried a new tack:

> ... the end of the war was followed by unprecedented manifestations of political openness on Saddam's part ... a public commitment to end the Ba'th monopoly on power, to establish a democratic multi-party system in Iraq, and to hold direct free elections for the country's presidency. These measures were accompanied by greater liberalisation of the Iraqi economy, a process begun in the mid-1970s and accelerated during the war. Price controls on all goods were lifted, and an attempt was made to attract capital from Gulf states and foreign companies. Many state-owned corporations were sold off to the private sector at very attractive prices, and there was much speculation about the eventual privatisation of all state enterprises except oil and the military industry.[45]

In addition, the government of Baghdad embarked on a policy of moderation, both within the Arab world and toward the West. As a sign of this, Iraq avoided its pre-war radical rhetoric and instead worked toward the creation of the Arab Co-operation Council (ACC), which counted Egypt, North Yemen, Jordan and Iraq as members. Iraq achieved a genuine diplomatic coup shortly thereafter, when King Fahd visited Iraq and concluded a non-aggression pact between the two countries. This pragmatic change of tactics boosted Iraq's image both at home and abroad. Even so, it failed to address the more important issue of its faltering economy.

The Economic Consequences of the War with Iran

Iraq is one of very few countries to have emerged within the span of less than a decade as a major militarised state. During the period of the war with Iran, it became a significant arms producer, surpassed in the Arab world only by Egypt. And Egypt, assisted by its traditional position of leadership in the Arab world (a position which kept it at war with Israel), had nevertheless developed its military industry only gradually, over a period of decades. Yezid Sayigh observes that:

> Iraqi military industrialisation is especially striking because it is the first instance of an Arab country building up its indigenous productive capability between 1984 and 1990, which indicates a high rate of financial and human investment and suggests the existence of a scientific and technical base sufficient to allow such rapid expansion.[46]

Iraq's invasions of its neighbours may in fact have been premeditated at the time of the inception of its earliest armaments programmes. In 1979, for example, it allocated a much larger share of its GDP to defence than did Canada, the USA, France, Turkey, India and Japan, all combined.[47] In the five years following 1984, Iraq spent $14.2 billion in hard currency on weaponry from Western countries, an amount which represented almost 60 per cent of its oil revenues.[48] Iraq's militarisation programme looked impressive and buttressed the confidence of the leadership, but it was surely both a snare and a delusion. Had the leaders been less confident of their battle capability, they would probably not have contemplated plunging their country into war against Iran, a neighbour with three times Iraq's population, a huge land mass, and an irrational leader.

In any case, Iraq's delusions of grandeur did not come cheaply. Not only was the direct financial cost enormous, in terms of expenditure on imported arms and the building of military industries and facilities, but a disproportionately high number of young men were lured into the armed services, a policy which inevitably damaged the nation's industries, since they could have been far more productive in the manufacturing sector. From 1980 to 1988, manpower increased in the army from 222,000 to an estimated 1 million: this represents a staggering increase of 350 per cent.[49]

This massive increase in manpower required a correspondingly high increase in military procurements. Iraq's arsenal became so extensive that, before the Gulf War, some experts were ranking Iraq as one of the top military states in the world. During the war with Iran the numbers of Iraqi tanks, for example, actually increased from 1900 in 1980 to 6300 in 1987/88, while those of Iraqi combat aircraft increased from 339 to more than 500.[50] Iraq's overall expenditure on arms increased from $1,180 million in 1973 to a peak in 1982 of approximately $25 billion. By the end of the war, that had decreased only to a mere $16.5 billion. These mind-boggling expenditures cover only the actual cost of the weaponry and do not include lost oil revenues, among other potential losses which will be referred to later. All in all, these expenditures turned oil-rich Iraq from one of the most prosperous countries in the region into the third largest debtor nation in the world (after the traditional Latin debtor nations, Brazil and Mexico, but ahead of Argentina), with estimated debts of $80 billion.[51] According to the Japanese Institute for Middle Eastern Economies, total Iraqi war losses from 1980 to 1985 amounted to $226 billion.[52]

To make matters worse, the major source of government revenue – oil – was bombed out of commission during the war. Syria decided to cut off the Iraqi oil pipeline running through its territory, and world oil prices dwindled. All of this added to the problems of Iraq's already devastated economy. On the other hand, the Saudis and also, ironically, the Kuwaitis, raised their oil production to include the unused Iraqi quota and gave the proceeds to Iraq in cash. While this was only a drop in the economic ocean, it was in addition to direct cash aid given to Iraq by its allies in the Gulf region.

Other problems persisted, as a direct outgrowth of the war with Iran. Prime among these was the 1 million-member Iraqi army, which had become a monster of the decision-makers' own creation. The need to feed it, and to keep it occupied, was a constant source of anxiety. Al-Jaber explains the dilemma:

> The socio-political time bomb was the army. At least three, perhaps four generations had been recruited, driven to the battlefields, and kept there for almost a decade. They had suffered the horrors and the agonies of a long and draining war, were deprived of the best years of youthful, active life, and became hungry for literally everything. In wartime a sense of national obligation elevated their spirits; in peacetime, a longing for lasting peace gathered momentum.[53]

Henceforth, oil would have played an important role in placating the army leadership with high-earning sinecures, the rank and file with bonuses. This time, however, Iraq faced a different situation. Oil production of almost two million barrels a day at $18 a barrel brought in approximately $12 billion annually. But the country's estimated debt of $80 to $100 billion required almost $10 billion annually to service it, leaving a country of almost 19 million people with around $2 billion to live on, a sharp reduction from its recent years of prosperity.

Immediately after the cease-fire between Iran and Iraq, the Iraqi military leadership found ways of keeping its men busy. Crushing the minority Kurds became a priority. In highly publicised reports seen all over the world, Saddam's army waged chemical war against the Kurds. The next natural enemy of Iraq was its arch-rival Syria, which had taken sides with Iran against Iraq. Thus, the state of Iraq found itself in the curious position of supporting right-wing Lebanese Christians led by General Michel Aoun, solely because they openly opposed the Syrian presence in Lebanon. And finally, as a part of a general effort to blame outsiders for Iraq's economic misery, it has been suggested that the government encouraged violent attacks against Egyptian workers in Iraq.[54]

The government's difficulties continued, however. British authorities confiscated what they thought might be tubes for building a super-gun. Iraq's nuclear capability prompted Israel to threaten to repeat its earlier humiliating bombing of Iraqi military facilities. Although Saddam threatened to burn half of Israel in retaliation, threats were all he had to offer. Western powers became increasingly apprehensive about Iraq's newly unpredictable role in the Middle East.

In the face of its undeniably declining creditworthiness, the Western nations curtailed their lending to Iraq. In this context the finance minister of France, M. Bérègovoy, later the French prime minister, made the following observation:

> We note that an enormous share of Iraq's GNP is currently being devoted to military industrialisation projects. We do not want to finance regional destabilisation. Nor will we issue any more export credit guarantees until the Iraqis make good on the debt rescheduling deal we worked out.[55]

The Ba'th regime began to crack under the weight of its obligations. The leadership realised that even with the most optimistic scenario, Iraq was still short of at least $10 billion annually.[56] Oil, the traditional saviour, was no longer a reliable revenue source. Kuwait and the United Arab Emirates were now openly challenging the quota allocated them.

As a result oil prices hovered at around $18 a barrel as they fought to gain market share. Foregoing further details of the dispute between Iraq and Kuwait, it will suffice here to repeat that Iraq under Saddam Hussein found the issue of oil with Kuwait, a country with which Iraq already had an unresolved territorial quarrel, a convenient pretext for war. The Iraqi leaders also, and most importantly, believed that the wealthy but powerless Kuwaitis would succumb to Iraq's demands.

A startling book by Saad al-Bazzaz, who is familiar with Saddam and many top Ba'thist officials, was released in 1992. Reviewed by the *Sunday Times* and the *Christian Science Monitor*, it presented candid revelations about what happened in Iraq just before the war, including the real motives behind the war. Economic considerations were primary, according to al-Bazzaz, and centred around Kuwait's disregard for OPEC quotas, and the financial damage that Kuwait's policies inflicted on Iraq.

According to al-Bazzaz, the war with Kuwait was inevitable. Had Iraq continued to let Kuwait flood the oil market, he maintains, Iraqi oil revenues would have not covered half its internal economic needs, let alone be able to service its debt.[57] The author argues further that:

> After eight years of attrition, Iraq cannot build on its previous economy with a high standard of living. It became necessary therefore, to find a permanent solution to the economic predicament, with its problem of debt, a solution which can only be geo-political which would provide new sources for the Iraqi economy.[58]

When al-Bazzaz asked Tariq Aziz to describe the philosophy behind the invasion of Kuwait, Aziz replied that the intention was to bring about a military coup, through which a new indigenous regime would replace the ruling family. As a result, Aziz said, 'in the ashes of the ruins we will build a politics of understanding rather than a politics of confrontation, to unite, to become one after the long separation, and finally, Iraq will be able to solve its economic problems with a lung open to the sea' (referring to the Shatt al-Arab waterway.)[59]

In a last-minute diplomatic attempt to contain the conflict as it escalated in June and July 1990, the Saudis hosted both parties at a meeting in Jedda on 1 August 1990. The two countries, each believing that the other was bluffing, sent only second-ranking politicians, who went through the motions of negotiation, arriving finally at an inevitable political impasse. Kuwait could now justifiably be regarded as a 'scape-goat' in the eyes of the Iraqi leadership. Iraq as a result – before any further attempt at reconciliation could be made – preempted world attempts at conciliation and invaded its neighbour, Kuwait.

Chapter 4

The Gulf War

Previous chapters have discussed the role of Saddam Hussein in causing the Gulf crisis of 1990, as well as the contribution made to the crisis by internal problems threatening the Iraqi state. It was argued that Saddam Hussein's personality made a significant contribution to the evolution of the crisis, and that the domestic problems facing the Iraqi state were also an important cause. This chapter will focus on conditions in the Gulf region in 1990 in the light of the international situation at that time – the 'framework of action' in which the crisis emerged.

There is little doubt that the sense of insecurity that prevailed among the leaders of states in the Gulf region in 1990, and the uncertainty that characterised the relationships of the Gulf states among themselves and with outside states, were the kind that are postulated by the recently discussed theories of international relations as conducive to the eruption of armed conflict. An anarchic system of self-help prevailed in the region. The actions of its states were consistent with a Hobbesian model of a situation where states that feel a strong sense of threat by other states promote the advancement of self-interest and security by any means, in the absence of a recognised sovereign authority. Changes in the international system, notably the end of the Cold War and the superpower confrontation, had also affected the Gulf region. It can be argued that a disequilibrium had subsequently emerged, in which no firm assumptions could be made about the behaviour of the United States or Soviet Union in the event of a crisis involving regional states that had previously been aligned on different sides of the Cold War.

The Gulf Region and the Anarchic International System

Unresolved border disputes are one of the major problems of an international system where there exists no sovereign authority, and

89

where many states do not recognise any binding system of international agreement or arbitration of disputes. Although by no means the only cause of the 1990 crisis, an unsettled border issue and an old Iraqi historical claim to Kuwait were major factors in Iraq–Kuwait relations well before the crisis.

Part of the problem dated back to the initial settlement of Middle East borders by Britain after the First World War. In negotiations about borders between Britain, Iraq, Kuwait and Saudi Arabia in 1922–23, the Iraq–Kuwait border was drawn up by Britain in line with a previous border designated in the Anglo–Ottoman Convention of 1913 (a convention never ratified by the Ottoman parliament).[1] This determination of borders left Iraq virtually landlocked, and assigned to Kuwait two strategic islands in the Gulf (Bubiyan and Warbah) that were considered by Iraq to be part of its territory. Iraqi governments, both during the period of the monarchy and the subsequent republic, constantly challenged this determination of the border.

Different Iraqi governments made an even broader historical claim to the effect that Kuwait had been a part of the Wilayat of Basra in Iraq under the Ottoman empire, and had been unjustifiably detached from Iraq only by British colonial power.[2] In the 1930s, King Ghazi of Iraq advanced a claim to Kuwait, and moved troops to the Iraq–Kuwait border. While this claim was not acted upon, a more serious crisis emerged in 1961 when Kuwait obtained independence, and the Iraqi ruler, General Abdul-Karim Qassim mobilised troops and formally announced Iraq's claim to Kuwait.

Under what appeared to be an imminent threat of force, Kuwait formally requested British assistance, to which the latter immediately responded with the dispatch of 5,000 British troops, on 30 June 1961.[3] Egypt's President Nasser, who then led the United Arab Republic, showed his concern at the situation and, along with other Arab countries including Saudi Arabia, dispatched a further 10,000 men to Kuwait as a deterrent force.[4] Although this ended the crisis for the time being, the border issue remained unresolved and likely to recur in any crisis between Iraq and Kuwait.

During the period between Qassim's claim to Kuwait and the Gulf crisis, Iraq sought to expand its regional influence by means other than territorial annexation. When President Sadat's signing of the Camp David Agreement in 1978 led to a decline in Egyptian influence in the

Arab world, Iraq sought to assume the mantle of Arab nationalism, with vigorous opposition to the Camp David Agreement and strong support for the Palestinian cause. A new opportunity for leadership in the Gulf region arose when the Shah of Iran was overthrown by the Islamic revolution in 1979. Saddam Hussein was able to take advantage of the fear caused by this revolution among the Gulf élites to establish closer relations with conservative Gulf states. When the Islamic government of Iran's determination to overthrow the Ba'th government of Iraq became clear, Saddam resorted to what amounted to a pre-emptive strike, deciding that a surprise war on a neighbour's territory was preferable to waiting for a war within Iraq's own borders.[5] The Iraqi leaders understood that they had no natural terrain for defence, so that a preventive war inside Iran's territory became even more attractive.[6]

This was a serious miscalculation, and led to a costly war of attrition, which Iraq did not – perhaps could not – win. The war had two major effects on Iraq's regional and international strength. First, by standing up to the radical and fundamentalist Shi'a revolutionary government of Iran, Iraq gained the support of virtually the entire international community, including the USA, Western Europe, and all the Arab nations except Syria and Libya. This international support included providing Iraq with arms and giving it access to financial as well as military intelligence.[7] As a result Iraq became militarily very powerful, with an arsenal which, according to some analysts, placed it among the five most powerful countries in the world. The second, and paradoxical result of the long war, was that its tremendous cost created such economic pressures on the Iraqi government, that it greatly increased the regime's political insecurity. Economic issues, such as oil pricing and the repayment of debts, were at the forefront of Iraq's relations with other countries, and were viewed as issues affecting the state's survival, not merely as routine problems.

Iraq saw itself as a major independent regional power, whose military strength entitled it to a commensurate political influence in the Gulf. As an exponent of Arab nationalism, of high oil prices, and of militant opposition to Israel, it adhered to objectives very different from those of the Western powers that dominated the international system, as well as those of its smaller, oil-rich neighbours. Its leadership was aware of this divergence of objectives, and constantly fearful of Western attempts to frustrate Iraqi policies and to weaken Iraq's capabilities. These fears became increasingly pronounced in Iraqi declarations in the period leading up to the Gulf crisis. Saddam Hussein's paranoia became apparent as the 1980s went on, and he repeatedly accused the international community of some sort of conspiracy against Iraq. A number of incidents convinced him that Western powers were predisposed to be hostile to Iraq. The 'Irangate' revelations showed that the American administration had been secretly selling weapons and military spare parts to Iran during the Iran–Iraq war. Although the objective had been to persuade Iran to use its influence to free American hostages held in Lebanon by pro-Iranian groups, Iraq interpreted the move as a sign of closer military co-operation between Washington and Tehran aimed – inevitably – at Baghdad.

In 1987 Saddam Hussein felt further threatened by the international scandal which followed when the Italian Banca Nazionale Lavoro (BNL) was discovered to be financing some of Iraq's military build-up by diverting a US line of credit intended for agricultural exports to Iraq.[8] Then a series of bombings occurred in Baghdad, directed at Western companies working on Iraqi super-weapon projects: these may well have been the work of Kurdish militants, but the Iraqi government preferred to blame the Israeli government, which had long put pressure on Western suppliers of weapons to Iraq.[9] In 1990, a British journalist of Iranian origin was caught investigating an explosion at a military base inside Iraq. Accused of being an agent of the Israeli security services, he was tried, found guilty, and executed. During the international outrage that followed his execution, the British, Greek and Turkish customs authorities discovered and confiscated shipments of what appeared to be materials for a 'super gun' project. The Voice of America described Saddam Hussein as a dictator, and the US State Department published the dismal human rights record of his administration. Parallels were made in the Western media between Saddam Hussein and the Romanian dictator Ceausescu, whose regime had recently been exposed as the Communist regimes of Eastern Europe lost control and collapsed.

Saddam Hussein's paranoia was heightened, according to Heikal,[10] when he allegedly received information from 'a friendly head of state, that a decision had been taken at the highest level in the West to treat Iraq as a new danger in the region'. Iraqi political rhetoric reminiscent of the 1960s now swung into action. Saddam hosted an Arab summit meeting in the Iraqi capital in May 1990, to discuss the West's anti-Iraq campaign. It was entitled 'Threat to Arab National Security' and the majority of the Arab heads of state attended. Excerpts from Saddam's opening address reflect the Iraqi leader's fears.

> ... It behoves us to declare clearly that if Israel attacks and strikes, we will strike powerfully. If it uses weapons of mass destruction against our nation, we will use against it the weapons of mass destruction in our possession ... The United States has demonstrated that it is primarily responsible for the aggressive and expansionist policies of the Zionist entity against the Palestinian Arab people and the Arab nation ...

> ... No Israeli aggression against the Arab nation can be isolated from the desire of American imperialism ... I use the word 'imperialism' only here. In fact I have not used this word for a long time. But when I saw the memorandum presented by the groups working at the US State Department, indicating that we should not use the word imperialism, I decided to use it.[11]

The increasingly desperate economic situation at home increased Iraq's sense of being under serious and threatening external pressures. Oil revenues had not lived up to Iraqi expectations as the ultimate saviour. Seeking a reason for this – other than the general turn-down in oil prices world-wide – Saddam turned on Kuwait and the United Arab Emirates, two countries which had exceeded their OPEC-allocated quotas for oil production. In a speech addressed to all Arab leaders, but with these two states clearly in mind, Saddam accused them of flooding the market so that prices had tumbled to as low as $7 per barrel; every dollar-per-barrel reduction, he claimed, meant the loss of $1 billion for Iraq.[12] Admitting his country's vulnerability, the Iraqi leader turned the economic issue into one of national security. He pointed out, accusingly:

> Frankly, war is fought not only with soldiers ... There are other means of conducting wars, economic means. We hope that our brethren who do not wish open war with Iraq will realise that this economic kind of war will not be tolerated any longer. We have come to a point beyond which we cannot go.[13]

After the invasion of Kuwait, the Iraqi foreign minister, Tariq Aziz, went even further, making an explicit connection between Iraq's faltering economy and its need to take action against those it perceived as responsible (e.g. Kuwait):

> The economic question was a major factor in triggering the current situation. In addition to the forty billion dollars in Arab debts, we owe at least as much to the West. This year's state budget required seven billion dollars for debt service, which was a huge amount, leaving us with only enough for basic services for our country. Our budget is based on a price of eighteen dollars a barrel for oil, but since the Kuwaitis began flooding the world with oil the price has gone down by a third ... When we met again – in Jidda, at the end of July – Kuwait said it was not interested in any change. We were desperate, and could not pay our bills for food imports. It was a starvation war. When do you use your military power to preserve yourself?[14]

Such assertions by Iraqi leaders confirm Gross Stein's hypothesis that:

> ... decisions to initiate war in the Middle East ... [are made by leaders who] are most likely to resort to force when they feel strategically vulnerable and anticipate that their strategic position will deteriorate further rather than improve in the future; when they are under intense political pressure either at home or from allies; and when they see little prospect for negotiation as an alternative strategy of conflict management.[15]

After making politically belligerent statements and hinting at military action against Kuwait, the Iraqi government made far-reaching demands. These included a long-term loan of $10 billion, the cancellation of Iraq's Iranian war debts, the cessation of Kuwaiti use of Rumeila (a disputed oilfield on the border) and the provision of a long-term agreement for Iraq to lease the Kuwaiti offshore islands, thus giving it access to the Gulf.

Not surprisingly, Kuwait did not accede to these demands. Instead, it audaciously reminded Iraq of the exact amount of its war debt, incurred over the eight years of its war with Iran. In response, requiring a show of force in order to give its demands credibility, the Baghdad government dispatched an estimated 30,000 troops to positions close to its Kuwaiti border on 21 July.

At this point, curiously, the United States issued a reminder to the world that there was no US treaty with the Kuwaiti government,[16] and followed this up with a visit by the US ambassador to the president of

Iraq on 25 July, only a week before the Iraqi invasion. This crucial meeting was to become very controversial, since some political observers subsequently argued that it might justifiably have been interpreted by Iraq as an American 'green light' for the invasion. Parts of the transcript of the meeting merit quoting in detail:

> *Saddam Hussein*: When planned and deliberate policy forces the price of oil down without good commercial reason, then that means another war against Iraq. Because ... military war kills people by bleeding them, and economic war kills their humanity by depriving them of their chance to have a good standard of living ... We gave rivers of blood in a war that lasted eight years ... We do not accept that anyone could injure Iraqi pride or the Iraqi right to have high standards of living.
>
> Kuwait and the UAE were at the front of this policy aimed at lowering Iraq's position ... On top of all that, while we were busy at war, the state of Kuwait has began to expand ... at the expense of our territory ...
>
> *Ambassador Glaspie*: [agreeing with him] We studied history at school. They taught us to say freedom or death ... but we have no opinion on Arab-Arab conflicts, like your border disagreement with Kuwait ... We hope you can solve this problem using any suitable methods via Klibi [the head of the Arab League] or via President Mubarak. All that we hope is that these issues are solved quickly. ... I received an instruction to ask you, in the spirit of friendship – not in the spirit of confrontation – regarding your intentions.[17]

During the meeting, Saddam reiterated his country's political, economic and territorial grievances, thus preparing the ground with a justification for military counter-measures should they be needed.

In a last-minute effort to defuse the situation, the Kuwaiti leadership agreed to meet the Iraqis, under the auspices of Saudi Arabia, in Jedda. At this meeting, although Kuwait agreed to the $500 million loan and to waiving the war debt, they insisted that the latter should remain on the books for accounting purposes. Thus Iraq was able to claim that the meeting had reached an impasse and was abruptly ended. A few hours later, on 1 August 1990, the Iraqis carried out their threat and invaded their neighbour.

In their own minds, the Iraqi leaders seem to have convinced themselves of their 'legitimate right' to invade Kuwaiti territory. They believed further that they had convinced others, in particular the USA, of this. They genuinely did not expect the UN or any other world organisation to intervene and settle the issue to their disadvantage.

One basis for this belief was that Saddam had already fought one major war, with Iran, without international intervention. In a world of self-help, anarchy, and disorder, he believed that the *ultima ratio* was the reason, judgement and force displayed by a state's leaders. This orientation toward a ruthless *realpolitik* was supported by his own experience in ascending to power in Iraq. Sheer brute force had successfully allowed him to climb the perilous ladder of the Iraqi leadership. Later, even more importantly, he had survived the longest and most devastating war in his country's short history, and emerged from the latter as *de facto* president for life, a man able to claim, with some justification that, by risking war with Iran, he had brought the Islamic Revolution to its knees. One vital lesson which he believed he had learned was that no credible enforcer came to the rescue of his victims, whether during his climb to power in Iraq, or during his war with Iran.

The Kuwaiti government's behaviour towards Iraq was similarly driven by what it perceived, in a world of self-help, anarchy and disorder, to be its best interest. Kuwait was, however, caught in the Security Dilemma. Thus, the effect of the entirely defensive Kuwaiti actions was to confirm Iraqi suspicions about the economically offensive Kuwaiti intentions. While the Kuwaiti leaders did not undertake any conventional defensive steps (i.e., the accumulation of military weapons likely to threaten Iraq), their diplomatic and economic intransigence played on Iraq's sense of insecurity, as articulated by its president.

An important strategic factor that influenced Saddam Hussein in his decision to make a pre-emptive attack was the exposed nature of Kuwait's geographical terrain, which makes it extremely difficult to defend. Kuwait shares 120 miles of border with Iraq; Kuwait City is only 75 miles from the border; a major Iraqi military base, south of Basra (Shuabia), is just 30 miles from the border and only 100 miles from Kuwait City itself.[18] Furthermore, the Kuwaiti army was at that time estimated at less than 16,000, and Kuwait had established no major defence agreement with an outside power, other than the GCC. Thus, Saddam was justified in assuming that a strong, surprise pre-emptive attack against Kuwait was very likely to succeed. His hope was that, in

an anarchic system of international relations, there would be no international response capable of forcing Iraq from Kuwait, and that the
eventual outcome of the invasion would be to Iraq's advantage.

With the benefit of hindsight it is now clear that, had the Kuwaiti
government understood the depth of Iraq's desperation and paranoia,
it might have averted the war. Saudi Arabia and Egypt are known to
have advised the Kuwaitis to act more flexibly in the negotiations
preceding the Iraqi invasion. Kuwait could, for example, have written
off a loan which its leaders, by their own admission, knew Iraq would
never repay. Equally, the Kuwaiti leadership could have understood and
sympathised with Iraq's geographical dilemma, especially its undesirable land-locked situation, and made a special arrangement regarding
Iraq's use of off-shore islands that left Kuwaiti sovereignty intact. Finally,
had Kuwait followed the example of several other Arab nations which
were sympathetic towards Iraq's economic crisis, and engaged in more
pragmatic financial discussions, the outcome would have been far less
expensive for Kuwait than the costs of war. This is not an attempt to
argue that the Kuwaiti government *should* have offered such concessions.
Acquiescence to the demands of opponents in the international arena is
a very complex matter. Questions of sovereignty, of independence, and
most importantly of the establishment of precedents may well have
been the overriding concerns of the Kuwaiti government.

Balance of Power

The Middle East and the Gulf region in particular seem to be an ideal
testing ground for theories of the balance of power and its effects –
especially the issue of whether or not the balance of power functions
to maintain the peace and security and independence of individual
states, or whether war turns out to be an instrument of the balance of
power. In no world region other than the Middle East do rapid shifts
in the balance of power occur so frequently. Friends turn to enemies
and vice versa virtually overnight, and solidarity blocs are formed one
day, only to be abrogated or totally ignored the next. In order to analyse
Iraq's invasion of Kuwait within a balance of power context, it is
necessary to put the always unsettled relationship between the two
countries in its historical perspective.

In the 1970s the Gulf region was relatively stable. Power was distributed fairly equally between two camps. On one side there existed what was known as the 'twin pillars', composed basically of Iran and Saudi Arabia, with their military power and economic resources, respectively, supported by (but by no means allied to) the USA and Western Europe. On the other side was Iraq, armed principally by the Russians through a military co-operation agreement, and perceived as pro-Soviet.

Both sides in the Middle East relied heavily upon their respective patrons. Saudi Arabia and Iran looked to the West for their arsenal, while Iraq imported huge numbers of Soviet-made weapons.[19]

Following the 1975 agreement between Iraq and Iran, signed in Algeria, Iraq seemed to move gradually toward a more pragmatic position, and became less antagonistic towards the lower Gulf states. This development affected the political balance of power significantly, in the direction of greater stability.

This relative equilibrium was shattered in 1977, when Egypt's President Sadat visited Jerusalem on a peace-making mission. The Arab countries rallied around Baghdad in a show of anti-Zionist solidarity, condemned Egypt and ostracised its president. Iraq found itself at the centre of Arab politics, its power enormously enhanced. Saddam Hussein – a man with life-long ambitions to lead the Arab world – eagerly seized the opportunity offered him.

Other, momentous changes followed, with long-term consequences for the Gulf area. The moderate pro-West monarchy of Iran was swept out of power in 1979, and replaced with a radical Islamic revolutionary government hostile not only to the West but also to the conservative Gulf states and Iraq. Meanwhile, the Soviet Union invaded Afghanistan, transforming the region's political landscape yet again.

In 1971, when the British withdrew from the Gulf, Iran under the Shah had emerged as the dominant naval power in the area, a situation which had prompted Iraq's 1975 agreement.[20] By the 1980s, however, Iran's power under its new Islamic regime had significantly diminished – principally because other states in the region, and particularly the USA, were unwilling to support a government of such extreme fundamentalist views. This gave Saddam Hussein the opportunity he had been seeking. He felt a genuine, personal need to regain the eastern part of the Shatt al-Arab, which he believed he had been coerced into signing away to Iran in 1975. As a result he sent Iraq's superior military might across the border into Iranian territory.

In danger of being caught up in a conflict between two powerful enemies over whom they had little or no control, the lower Gulf states enacted several sitting-on-the-fence measures. Since Iran was mounting a major propaganda campaign against their conservative monarchies, they decided to come to the aid of Iraq financially, but at the same time they remained discreetly unwilling to let Iraq use their ports and airfields for military purposes.[21] Certain other countries in the region, however – in particular Israel, Syria, and Libya – backed Iran rather more whole-heartedly, so that the conflict bred a complex set of alliances which did not break down neatly along Arab vs. Iranian lines.[22]

In 1981, a year after the Iran–Iraq war broke out, the six Arab Gulf states formalised their political and military co-operation into what became known as the Gulf Co-operation Council (GCC). One of the Council's most significant achievements, according to Ursula Braun, was the creation of the Gulf Rapid Deployment Force, with a small contingent of highly-trained troops located in the northern part of Saudi Arabia under Saudi command.[23] As Anthony Cordesman points out, through this formal institution, the six countries were able to create a regional security force, employing advanced technology to substitute for their lack of readily available manpower.[24]

During the war between Iraq and Iran a new, three-way balance of power became established, with the emergence of three distinct political forces; Socialist Ba'th Republicanism; Radical Islamic Republicanism; and Traditional Islamic Monarchism. Ehteshami and Tripp explain how this complex conjuncture emerged:

> First, it occurred at a time of financial crisis in virtually all the Gulf states. Secondly, it was fuelled by war and was not run purely for prestige and competition. Thirdly, and perhaps most notably, we see, with the end to the Iran–Iraq war, three distinct identities emerging in the Gulf, each trying to function independently of the others but also to co-operate with the others to the extent that the fundamental interests of each are not threatened. Since 1979, and in particular since the GCC was formed in 1981, these three political forces ... have emerged in their own right.[25]

Of those countries not directly concerned with the conduct of the war, only Kuwait was affected directly. On several occasions, in an effort to discourage the small emirate from assisting Iraq financially,

Iran launched some of its Chinese-made Scuds into Kuwait's territory. And later, for the same reason, as the war raged toward its end, Kuwaiti oil tankers became targets for Iran – so much so that at one point Kuwait felt its country to be virtually under a blockade.[26] This proved to be an Iranian misjudgement, however, since it prompted the two superpowers to intervene. The Soviets chartered a number of their own tankers to Kuwait, and the USA provided armed naval escorts for Kuwaiti tankers, with the inevitable effect of altering the balance of power in Iraq's favour. By the time the Iran–Iraq war ended with a cease-fire in 1988, a change in the distribution of power had taken place. Iraq, with its military might virtually intact, emerged as the pre-eminent power in the region, to the chagrin of virtually everyone. Confident of its power, Iraq spearheaded efforts to revive the now defunct Arab Co-operation Council, which included Egypt, Jordan, Iraq, and North Yemen. Iraq also flexed its military muscle in Lebanon, and engaged in ominous political rhetoric against the USA and Israel. In an effort to counter its arch-rival, the ruling Ba'th party of Syria, Iraq supported the right-wing Lebanese Christian forces under the self-styled leadership of Michel Aoun. Finally, it adopted an aggressive stance against its small neighbour, Kuwait, and when all attempts at political extortion ended in an impasse, it resorted to military invasion.

This exposed the weakness of the GCC, despite its Rapid Deployment Force. The result was the intervention of a UN-backed military coalition, headed by the USA, in order to establish a new balance of power in the region. The resulting conflict left Iraq seriously weakened, the almost automatic corollary being that Iran emerged as the new power to watch.

It is plausible to argue that the Iraqi invasion was one of the consequences of the disequilibrium in the regional balance of power that had resulted from, first, the changed international orientation of Iran under its revolutionary regime, which was one of the causes of the Iran–Iraq war, and second, from the end of the Cold War, which meant that states in the Gulf region were no longer part of a polarised international system. Without the Iran–Iraq war, it is unlikely for reasons discussed above that there would have been an Iraqi invasion of Kuwait; and if a Cold War situation had existed, in which US–Soviet tensions were acute, it is difficult to imagine Saddam Hussein's Iraq, a client of the Soviet Union, invading a major oil-producing state friendly to the United States.

Saddam Hussein clearly misunderstood the willingness of the United States to intervene on behalf of a friendly, oil-producing state in the post-Cold War era. Like most observers of the situation at the time, he also failed to predict the strength, diversity and cohesion of the international alliance that was formed to confront the Iraqi invasion. This opposition raised the possibility that a more effective international role could be played in dealing with world conflicts, and that international law could become the basis for their resolution.

The Gulf War and International Law

The Iraqi invasion of Kuwait raised major issues of international law. The armed UN intervention that resulted was justified in terms of international law, although a controversy ensued, centred principally on the accusation that the major powers were invoking international law in support of military action simply because their oil supplies were threatened. There was also widespread concern in religious circles that the attack mounted by the US-led coalition might not meet the traditional 'just war' criteria. In particular, could any war be considered 'morally defensible'[27] before all other means of settling the dispute had been exhausted?

The invasion was an unambiguous violation of the fundamentals of international law governing the behaviour of states. It provoked almost unanimous world condemnation, through the medium of the UN. Unprecedented cohesion was shown by the multi-ethnic, multi-cultural military coalition opposed to the Iraqi invasion. The aggression was clearly seen not only in legalistic terms as a violation of the formal rules of international society, but also in emotional terms, as an assault upon a people, their everyday life and their physical survival.[28]

The degree to which the military actions of the coalition met the different criteria laid down in international law needs to be examined. Article 51 of the UN charter is clear in its affirmation of 'the inherent rights of individual or collective self-defence, if an armed attack occurs against a member of the United Nations, until the Security Council has taken measures necessary to maintain international peace and security'. In order for a UN military intervention to come within the framework of this provision it is necessary for one of the concerned parties to request assistance. David Scheffer unravels the intricate legalities surrounding the coalition's counter-offensive:

No one would have credibly contested on legal grounds a US counterattack against the Iraqi army if it had occurred immediately – within hours or days – following the invasion and if Kuwait or, if circumstances required it, Saudi Arabia had requested such assistance. Nor would there have been any argument if the Iraqi army had invaded Saudi Arabia and coalition forces had acted in self-defence, even to the extent of liberating Kuwait and neutralising the Iraqi threat to the region during the ensuing conflict. Article 51 clearly permits rapid unilateral or collective responses to aggression without waiting for a Security Council decision.[29]

After the Security Council met to consider the Iraqi invasion, it determined that an Iraqi violation had indeed occurred, and called for Iraq's immediate and unconditional withdrawal. When Iraq failed to comply, on 6 August the Security Council imposed economic sanctions by passing Resolution 661.[30] Such measures included a ban on all imports and exports to Iraq, the protection of Kuwaiti assets, and an immediate halt to any international funding of Iraqi government projects, save those payments intended for medical supplies and foodstuffs. Shortly thereafter, another resolution was approved, allowing the use of force against shipping to and from Iraq.[31]

When it was clear that economic sanctions and diplomatic fury might not be able to reverse the Iraqi invasion, the UN Security Council on 29 November passed Resolution 678, which authorised the use of military force against Iraq. Twelve members voted in favour; China abstained, while Cuba and Yemen voted against it.[32] About six weeks later, the US Congress passed a bill which gave President Bush the authority to engage in war. It was only after these two important legalistic moves that war became virtually inevitable.

The issue of whether the war could be considered a just war sparked a vigorous international debate. Politicians, academics, and commentators were uncertain as to whether or not it was appropriate and 'just' to go to war before the economic sanctions had been given ample time in which to succeed or fail. President Bush attempted to clarify the issue, drawing heavily upon the vocabulary of the Christian concept of a just war enshrined in international law, when he asserted 'we know that this is a just war, and we know that, God willing, this a war that we will win.'[33]

It is useful here to examine whether the principle of *Jus Ad Bellum* applies to the Gulf War conflict.

The concept of a just war grows out of the Western tradition of *Jus natural* (natural law) and *Jus gentium* (law of nations). Christian philosophers such as St Augustine and St Thomas Aquinas gave the Church's support to the concept, one that prohibits the use of force (war) in all except the most exceptional situations – principally those where justice is perceived to be on the victim's side. Elaborating upon the criteria set down by Aquinas, William O'Brien enumerates the conditions under which war may be deemed permissible.[34] First, a just war may be waged only by '*competent authority*'. O'Brien makes the point that in ancient times all the forces of authority within a nation overlapped and so were all intrinsically 'competent'. Today, when this is not so, 'competent authority' must be defined and he offers this definition: 'on the order of public authority for public purposes'. Thus, when a leader who rules by force decides for whatever reason he may have (i.e., personal vendetta) to wage war, his action is neither legitimised by public authorisation nor serves the public good, so that the war clearly has not been undertaken by O'Brien's 'competent authority'.

O'Brien's second criterion mirrors that of St Thomas Aquinas: war must be waged for 'a just cause'. O'Brien defines a 'just' cause thus: (i) it must be 'serious and weighty' (ii) the war must be defensive (iii) proportionality must exist 'between the just ends and the means' which can only occur when 'the probable good expected to result from success is weighed against the probable evil' which the war may cause and (iv) war should be waged only as a last resort, where all peaceful options have been tried and have failed.

O'Brien himself admits the difficulty of applying such idealistic and morally-based criteria within today's political climate: nevertheless, although deception and extreme violence are widely practised and the United Nations Organisation is perceived as a paper tiger, most states are sufficiently concerned with their world image to be at some pains to construct at least a semblance of international legality around their actions.

Was the coalition's attack on Iraqi positions *permissible*, a *justifiable* and *proportional* use of force on the victim's side by a *competent authority* as a *last resort*, and under *serious and weighty* circumstances?

Just cause: Neither the UN nor any other international entity used the phrase 'a just war' or attempted to define it. One easy modern formula would simply hold that a just war is one which is consistent with the criteria laid down in the UN charter.[35] Just cause requires the restoration of the *status quo ante*, which includes among other considerations, the removal of the threat of the aggressor.[36]

Proportionality: In this case, did the probable good expected from successful intervention outweigh the probable evil intervention might cause? This has proved a very difficult question to answer. Indeed, it is difficult to judge what the intervention achieved, even today. Had the Coalition failed to reverse the Iraqi expansion, the consequences would undeniably have been grave. Even so, George Wiegel for one suggests that wars are never legitimate and the destruction they leave behind is to be abhorred.[37] It is always greater than any benefits; how can we accurately measure the value of a country's independence except in terms of body counts?[38]

The inadequacy of the application of the proportionality criterion to the war in the Gulf was well expressed by *La Civilta Cattolica* which often reflects the views of the Vatican:

> It was waged for a 'just' cause – the liberation of Kuwait from the Iraqi invasion. But by its own inexorable logic it led, first of all, to the systematic destruction of Iraq. We are told that ninety thousand tons of bombs were dropped, leaving an incalculable number of civilian dead and wounded. And then the war led to the destruction of the Iraqi army, so as to prevent Iraq from constituting a military danger in the future. Thus the liberation of Kuwait was purchased at the price of destroying a country and killing hundreds of thousands of people. At this point, can we still talk about a 'just war?' Shouldn't we say instead that 'just wars' can't exist because even when just causes come into play, the harm wars do by their very nature is so grave and horrendous that they can never be justified in the forum of conscience?[39]

There was collateral damage which seemed to go beyond the 'just war' criteria. The bombing of the water, electricity and sewage services in Iraq did great harm to the civilian population. Also although the Coalition went to great lengths to show how its 'smart' bombs selected their targets and how its cruise missiles followed the street signs in Baghdad, high Iraqi civilian casualties were caused, even though their extent is unknown.

Competent authority: The action followed a process of consultation and debate, both within and outside the formal structure of the UN. The two most important results of this consultation process, which seem to meet the competent authority criterion, were first, the approval of the US Congress as a democratically elected body which authorises a democratically elected president, and second, the vigorous debate within the international community's most prestigious organisation, the UN, which resulted in firm resolutions from the UN Security Council.

Last Resort: Given the nature of the conflict, this criterion is also difficult to satisfy. The Iraqis were so formidably armed that the UN's economic sanctions would have taken a very long time to have a significant effect. Even so, many observers – including the Archbishop of Canterbury, Robert Runcie – believed passionately that economic sanctions should be tried for as long as a year before any resort to force.[40] (This view ignored the dilemma of the Kuwaitis, suffering under a brutal Iraqi occupation.) The former chairman of the Joint Chiefs of Staff, Admiral William Crowe, commented that:

> It would be a sad commentary if Saddam Hussein, a two-bit tyrant who sits on 17 million people and possesses a gross national product of $40 billion, proved to be more patient than the United States, the world's most affluent and powerful nation.[41]

Kimberly Elliott, Gary Hufbauer and Jeffrey Schott, who are familiar with economic sanctions, argued in the *Washington Post* that:

> A review of the 115 cases since 1914 shows that success was achieved 40 times, when economic sanctions were threatened or imposed against individual countries ... The current UN sanctions are by far the strongest and most complete ever imposed against any country by other nations. These comparisons strongly suggest that, given time, the UN economic boycott can achieve by peaceful means what Bush and his advisers say can only be won by force.[42]

President Bush, on the other hand, maintained that 'extraordinary diplomatic efforts' had been made and exhausted when a special, high-level meeting was held in Geneva between Tariq Aziz and James Baker on 9 January 1991, but failed to make progress. Supporters of this viewpoint argued that, with Iraq firmly and cynically established in Kuwait, there was virtually no limit to Saddam Hussein's capacity to use delaying tactics in meetings and to parry diplomatic or economic measures against him.

Serious and Weighty: There is no question that the circumstances and nature of the war were serious and weighty. Also, since the 'just war' doctrine traditionally requires a war to be waged defensively rather than offensively, the war against Saddam's Iraq can be justified by the classic notion that what the Iraqis did was evil. Therefore, Kuwait was wrongly seized, and its recapture by the coalition forces can be considered self-defence, as can any reasonable punishment meted out to the regime of Saddam Hussein.[43]

Thus the criteria of the traditional 'just war' doctrine can be argued persuasively either way.

The Gulf War as an Instance of Collective International Action

In addition to the issue of the justice of the Gulf War an important political and legal question is whether it represented a unique instance of international intervention, or whether it reflected a new determination to implement the principles of international law in order to create, in President Bush's words, 'a New World Order'.

A strong argument can be made that the Gulf intervention will eventually be seen as an extremely rare instance of international protection of a small state. Arend and Beck point out that 'In the history of the United Nations, the Security Council has authorized the use of force against an aggressor in only two conflicts: the Korean War and the Gulf War.'[44] Few would maintain that these two conflicts were the only cases of international aggression in the period since the Second World War.

The fact that there was a Security Council intervention in each of the Korean and Kuwaiti cases owes much to two characteristics that the Korean War and Gulf War shared. First, in each case, the United States regarded its vital interests as threatened by aggression against a friendly country, and it was willing to make a massive military deployment to prevent the aggression. Second, the Soviet Union did not use its power of veto in the Security Council, for very different reasons in each case. At the time of the Korean War it was boycotting the Security Council in protest against the refusal to admit the Peoples' Republic of

China to membership of the United Nations. At the time of the Gulf crisis, the Cold War was already over, and the Soviet Union was interested in cooperation with the United States to bring about a more peaceful world order in which the Soviet Union could enjoy the prosperity that had eluded it; it was not willing to stand behind a Middle East ally engaged in aggression.

The Security Council interventions in Korea and the Gulf were thus responses to an unusual conjecture of international circumstances. There was a threat to the vital interests of a major power, the United States; and the international conjecture allowed the United Nations Security Council to sponsor action against the source of this threat. The systematic enforcement of international law would, however, require that aggression be countered by Security Council intervention regardless of whether or not it is directed against the vital interests of a great power. There is no evidence of the significant development since the Gulf War of an international willingness or capability to intervene with massive military force against regional aggressors in such circumstances. Despite widespread condemnation of Serbian actions against Bosnia, no effective international support has been offered to Bosnia. Although an intervention was authorised by the United Nations in the civil conflict in Somalia, this was limited to the protection of humanitarian aid supplies, not aimed at correcting the root causes of the conflict in the country. Moreover, in the states that are most likely to supply the military power for future interventions, there is no indication of strong political support for military interventions overseas in situations where vital state interests are not threatened.

The Gulf War was the only one of the two cases cited by Arend and Beck where there was substantial agreement among major powers over the need to confront aggression. A lack of such agreement is a major obstacle to any sanctions against aggression. Since it is possible for any of the five permanent members to veto measures by the Security Council, there is no chance of a repetition of the international response to the Gulf crisis in any situation where the aggressor is one of the five permanent members of the Council, or a close ally of one of these powers. Although in 1990–91, China and the Soviet Union were sensitive to the vital interests of the United States and Europe in the security of world oil supplies, few regional conflicts affect vital international interests in the same way (and few start with such a blatant act of aggression as Saddam's invasion of Kuwait). In many other conflicts, the permanent members of the Security Council are likely to disagree on the allocation of blame. As O'Brien points out:

> Even though an enforcement action was carried out by the United States and other members of the U.N. coalition against Iraq, the status of U.N. war-decision law may not be fundamentally or permanently changed ... One can think of other possible conflicts, e.g., between India and Pakistan, where Security Council members and other members might support different belligerents. Their vetoes and other votes might block Security Council action.[45]

In the world after the Gulf War, there is little reason to believe that small states that are marginal to the interests of the United States or other major powers are safer or better protected against an aggressor than before the Gulf War.

Conclusion

Throughout his book, *Man, the State and War*, Waltz maintains that the causes of war cannot be reduced to one single factor. To say that the causes of the Gulf War are complex, however, does not mean that they are not also specific. The point of this study has been to demonstrate that there was a specific and complex set of factors which led to the war.

We have seen, first of all, that it is important to examine the extent to which the Gulf War might indeed be considered to be 'Saddam's war'. It can even be argued that a different Iraqi leader would not have taken on the invasion of Kuwait, nor led his country into the subsequent war. The personality of Saddam Hussein was, therefore, a key cause of the 1990–91 Gulf crisis. His predecessors, although possibly also tempted by Kuwaiti oil wealth, had been too prudent to promote Iraqi claims to the extent of launching open hostilities against Kuwait. Our investigation of Saddam Hussein's personal and political history has demonstrated how a certain kind of leader can influence the course of history.

For a leader to have this effect, there must exist a political system that allows individual leaders to be extremely powerful. The specific nature of the state of Iraq, therefore, constituted an important part of Saddam's decision to invade Kuwait. Iraq entered the Gulf crisis with a particular set of problems and vulnerabilities resulting from its post-Ottoman legacy. Iraq had been created in a post-colonial settlement that left disputed borders; maintaining internal unity had been a struggle because of the diversity of ethnic groups with transnational ties and potential foreign supporters; it was surrounded by potentially hostile neighbours with which it had little in common; and it faced major economic problems. The insecurity and pressures arising from this predicament helped to move Iraq toward an aggressive foreign policy. This suggests that the particular combination of internal instability and dictatorial government with a certain type of autocratic leader, such as Saddam Hussein, may be devastating.

Despite the importance of these factors, it is extremely unlikely that the invasion of Kuwait would have taken place had it not been for the anarchic situation that prevailed in the international arena at the time. In the earlier Cold War period, with relatively clear limitations on the ability of a superpower client to invade a client of the rival superpower, a state like Iraq, which was tied to the Soviet Union, would not have invaded a state like Kuwait, which was friendly to the West, and a key oil-producing country. In the post-Cold War vacuum which prevailed in the Gulf region, there was much greater room for error and miscalculation. Saddam Hussein calculated that, without a perceived Soviet threat in the region, the United States might overlook the invasion of one of the small Gulf states; and the United States, which was itself vague about its commitment to Kuwait – and certainly not as clearly committed to Kuwait as it was to the major oil producer of the region, Saudi Arabia – had not defined its post-Cold War role in the Gulf region.

The Gulf war will always be a dark spot in Arab political history. Unlike a number of previous defeats, whose enormity was concealed by revolutionary leaders, the war was widely broadcast on Arab television. Painful scenes from it have been etched in Arab memories: young men dead on the battlefield; Iraqi troops surrendering to Italian newsmen and kissing the hands of American marines; and the humiliating cease-fire agreement signed by the Iraqis with the coalition forces on Iraqi territory. The damage caused by the hostilities was immense, as illustrated by the burning oil wells of Kuwait, and the destruction of targets in Iraq. There was a terrible loss of life. This was not a war with little impact, that might be soon forgotten, but one that ensured that the region would never be the same again.

The war reversed the situation that had arisen after the Iran–Iraq war, when Iraq emerged as the preponderant power in the Gulf region, in a manner threatening to its neighbours. As a direct consequence of the war, Iran seemed to assume the role of the new threatening power in the region. On the other hand, as a result of King Fahd's decision to allow the coalition forces to operate in Saudi Arabia, which risked his country's prestige and his personal rule, Kuwait had been saved.

The Iraqi defeat crushed the empty rhetoric that had prevailed in Arab politics. A new sense of realism led to Arab–Israeli peace talks, and ultimately to the historic Palestinian–Israeli peace accord, which could probably not have been contemplated in an Arab world where Iraq was the pre-eminent military power.

Some of the arguments of this book have highlighted aspects of the international relations prevailing in 1990 that helped to cause the war. For the establishment of peace, it is clearly important that there should be no recurrence of a situation where miscalculations such as Saddam Hussein's decision to invade Kuwait arise from a weak regional system of deterrence that results in a lack of knowledge about the consequences of violent actions. Small countries could also be protected by the establishment of strong mechanisms for the enforcement of international law, although the failure of the United States and Western powers in Bosnia left little ground for immediate optimism about the possibility of this development. The Gulf crisis also showed that unresolved border disputes, such as that between Kuwait and Iraq, can erupt violently; there is a good argument for major efforts to resolve such disputes before they lead to a major crisis.

It is also clear that certain kinds of state systems are less conducive than others to the maintenance of peace. A tyrannical regime with aspirations to regional hegemony and sharp insecurities about its neighbours is likely to be a threat to regional peace. Moreover, the kind of leadership that often flourishes in such states is likely to be experienced in the art of political violence, and uninhibited about the use of force at home and abroad if major benefits can thereby be obtained. On the other hand, governments with commitments to political participation and human rights are subject to constraints as a result of their own political values and the opinions of their populations. A spread of political systems of this kind could be beneficial for the cause of peace.

The Gulf War was a tragedy for the Arab world. In the immediate postwar period, there was a greater concern among Arabs with the establishment of peace in the region and with effective means of promoting social and economic development in different parts of the Arab world. A continuation of this trend would hold out hope that the Gulf War was a turning point following which new and improved relations could be established among the Arab states and peoples.

Notes

Introduction

1 Mohamed H. Heikal, *Illusions of Triumph: An Arab View of the Gulf War* (London, 1992) p 31.

2 For the purposes of this book, the Gulf War will be considered to have begun with Iraq's invasion of Kuwait on 2 August 1990. A useful consideration of both the immediate and the historical origins of the border conflict between Kuwait and Iraq can be found in Ibrahim Ibrahim, 'Sovereign States and Borders in the Gulf Region: An historical perspective', in Ibrahim Ibrahim, (ed.), *The Gulf Crisis: Background and Consequences* (Washington D.C., 1992).

3 Kenneth Neal Waltz, *Man, the State, and War: A Theoretical Analysis* (New York, 1959).

Chapter 1 Kenneth Waltz on War and Peace

1 Kenneth Waltz, *Man, the State and War* (New York, 1959), p 2; The author himself suggests this title for his book: 'To borrow the title of a book by Mortimer Adler, our subject is "How to Think about War and Peace".' The chapters that follow are, in a sense, essays in political theory.

2 It should be pointed out that the structure of analysis which Waltz puts forth in his book has been criticized by Stanley Hoffman. His primary reservation comes from the distinct separation of the three concepts of Waltz's framework. Hoffman argues that as a result of the sharp division between the concepts of the individual, the state and the international system, the unity of the philosophy as a whole is distorted and even destroyed. cf Stanley Hoffman, *The State of War: Essays on the Theory and Practice of International Politics* (New York, 1965) p 57.

3 Waltz: *Man, the State and War*, p 3.

4 Waltz: *Man, the State and War*, p 16.

5 Waltz: *Man, the State and War*, p 21.

6 Waltz: *Man, the State and War*, p 18.

7 Waltz: *Man, the State and War*, pp 18–19.

8 Waltz: *Man, the State and War*, p 20.

9 Waltz: *Man, the State and War*, pp 32–3.

10 Waltz: *Man, the State and War*, pp 32–3.

11 Waltz: *Man, the State and War*, pp 33–4.

12 Waltz: *Man, the State and War*, p 39.

13 Waltz: *Man, the State and War*, pp 40–1.

14 Waltz: *Man, the State and War*, p 95.

15 Waltz: *Man, the State and War*, p 120.

16 Waltz: *Man, the State and War*, p 160.

17 Waltz: *Man, the State and War*, p 160.

18 Waltz: *Man, the State and War*, p 182.

19 To illustrate this point in his work, *A Discourse on the Origin of Inequality*, Rousseau uses the example of the stag-hunt: Five men, living during what Rousseau calls the early state of nature, come together in need of finding food. They agree to cooperate in hunting down a stag, which will provide enough food for five men. One hare, however, would feed any single one of the men. Eventually, a hare comes along and one of the men grabs it. Because of his distraction, the stag escapes and the other four men go hungry. cf Waltz pp 167–8.

20 Waltz: *Man, the State and War*, p 183; Cited from Rousseau, *A Lasting Peace*, tr. Vaughan, pp 46–8.

21 Waltz: *Man, The State and War* , p 183.

22 Waltz: *Man, The State and War*, pp 184–5.

23 Waltz: *Man, the State and War*, p 185; cited from Rousseau, *A Lasting Peace*, tr. Vaughan, pp 38–9.

24 Waltz: *Man, the State and War*, pp 198–200.

25 Waltz: *Man, the State and War*, pp 204–5.

26 Waltz refers to balance of power politics as a 'fascinating "game"' at the end of his book (p 223) and explains that he means no frivolity by that term. Much of his book, as we have seen, is based on the idea that the rules of politics are very similar in function to the rules of games.

27 Waltz: *Man, the State and War*, pp 209–10.

28 Waltz published his book in the 1950s and his emphasis on the West in international politics is clear. A concern for American–Soviet relations is also a strong theme. That there is a world-wide balance-of-power amongst all states can be inferred from Waltz's argument. His emphasis on the West in his political analysis is, however, important and requires noting.

29 Waltz: *Man, the State and War*, pp 219–20.

30 Waltz: *Man, the State and War*, pp 222–3.

31 Waltz: *Man, the State and War*, p 229.

32 Waltz: *Man, the State and War*, pp 229–30.

33 Waltz: *Man, the State and War*, pp 233–4.

34 Waltz points out that this perspective is put further by the Federalist Papers, especially those written by Hamilton and Jay; cf Waltz p 237.

35 Waltz: *Man, the State and War*, p 238.

36 Waltz: *Man, the State and War*, p 238.

Chapter 2 Saddam Hussein

1 Majid Khadduri, *Arab Personalities in Politics* (Washington DC, 1981) p 9.

2 Khadduri: *Arab Personalities*, p 11.

3 Simon Henderson, *Instant Empire: Saddam Hussein's Ambition for Iraq* (San Fransisco, 1991) p 51.

4 N.C. Menon, *Mother of Battles: Saddam's Folly* (Delhi, 1991), p 4.

5 Menon: *Mother of Battles*, p 5.

6 John Bulloch and Harvey Morris, *Saddam's War: The Origins in the Kuwait Conflict and the International Response* (London, 1991), p 31.

7 Menon: *Mother of Battles*, p 5.

8 Efraim Karsh and Inari Rautsi, *Saddam Hussein: A Political Biography* (New York, 1991), p 9.

9 Karsh and Rautsi: *Saddam Hussein*, p 9.

10 Karsh and Rautsi: *Saddam Hussein*, p 16.

11 Bulloch and Morris: *Saddam's War*, p 32.

12 Majid Khadduri, *Socialist Iraq: A Study in Iraqi Politics since 1968* (Washington DC, 1978), p 74.

13 Karsh and Rautsi: *Saddam Hussein*, p 7.

14 Henderson: *Instant Empire*, p 54.

15 Phebe Marr, *The Modern History of Iraq* (Oxford, 1985), p 128.

16 Fuad Matar, *Saddam Hussein: The Man, the Cause, and the Future* (London, 1981), p 31.

17 Karsh and Rautsi: *Saddam Hussein*, p 14.

18 Henderson: *Instant Empire*, p 53.

19 Henderson: *Instant Empire*, p 10.

20 Henderson: *Instant Empire*, p 59.

21 Karsh and Rautsi: *Saddam Hussein*, p 10.

22 Karsh and Rautsi: *Saddam Hussein*, p 15.

23 Karsh and Rautsi: *Saddam Hussein*, p 15.

24 Henderson: *Instant Empire*, p 53.

25 Khadduri: *Socialist Iraq*, p 73.

26 Judith Miller and Laurie Mylroie, *Saddam Hussein and the Crisis in the Gulf* (New York, 1990) p 24.

27 Karsh and Rautsi: *Saddam Hussein*, p 179.

28 Bulloch and Morris: *Saddam's War*, p 29.

29 Amir Iskandar, *Saddam Hussein: An Official Biography*, p 29.

30 Iskandar: *Saddam Hussein*, p 45.

31 Iskandar: *Saddam Hussein*, p 219.

32 Adel Darwish and Gregory Alexander, *The Secret History of Saddam's War: Unholy Babylon* (New York, 1991) p 201.

33 Bernard Reich (ed.), *Political Leaders of the Contemporary Middle East and North Africa: A Biographical Dictionary* (New York, 1990) p 241.

34 Reich: *Political Leaders*, p 202.

35 Reich: *Political Leaders*, p 243.

36 Reich: *Political Leaders*, p 74.

37 Saddam Hussein, *Saddam Hussein on Current Events in Iraq*, translated by Khalid Kishtainy (London, 1977).

38 As a young boy, the author lived in a small city in Saudi Arabia on the Yemeni border. He recalls vividly how passionately people in that region responded to Nasser's political speeches.

39 Saddam Hussein: *Current Events in Iraq*, p xi.

40 Mansfield, Peter, 'Saddam Hussein's political thinking: the comparison with Nasser', in Tim Niblock (ed.), *Iraq: The Contemporary State* (London, 1982) p 63.

41 Hanna Batatu, *The Old Social Classes and the Revolutionary Movements of Iraq: A Study of Iraq's Old Landed and Commercial Classes and Its Comunists, Ba'thists and Free Officers* (Princeton, 1978).

42 Matar, Fuad, *Saddam Hussein, the Man, the Cause and the Future* (London, 1981) p 49.

43 Karsh and Rautsi: *Saddam Hussein*, pp 110–11.

44 Henderson: *Instant Empire*, p 77.

45 Darwish and Alexander, *The Secret History*, p 197.

46 Samir Khalil, *Republic of Fear: The Politics of Modern Iraq* (Berkeley, 1989) p 110.

47 Khalil: *Republic of Fear*, p 110.

48 Henderson: *Instant Empire*, p 3.

49 Matar: *Saddam Hussein*, p 235.

50 King Hussein of Jordan and King Hassan of Morocco, for example, trace their ancestry to the Quraish, the Prophet's tribe. Other leaders in the Gulf, including those of Saudi Arabia, Kuwait, the U.A.E., Bahrain, Oman

and Qatar are all believed to come from noble tribal families, which adds to their political legitimacy.

51 Khalil: *Republic of Fear*, p 115.

52 Bulloch and Morris: *Saddam's War*, p 45.

53 Bernard Lewis (ed.), *Islam, from the Prophet Muhammad to the Capture of Constantinople* (London, 1976) pp 23–4.

54 Darwish and Alexander: *The Secret History*, p 215.

55 Amatzia Baram, 'Saddam Hussein: A political profile', *The Jerusalem Quarterly*, no. 17 (1989) p 143.

56 Bulloch and Morris: *Saddam's War*, p 71.

57 Darwish and Alexander: *The Secret History*, p 211.

58 Matar: *Saddam Hussein, the Man*, p 240.

59 Matar: *Saddam Hussein, the Man*, p 256.

60 Matar: *Saddam Hussein, the Man*, p 256.

61 Khadduri: *Socialist Iraq*, p 75.

62 Ofra Bengio (ed.), *Saddam Speaks on the Gulf Crisis: A Collection of Documents* (Tel Aviv: Moshe Dayan Center for Middle Eastern and African Studies, 1992) p 331.

63 Matar: *Saddam Hussein, the Man*, p 229.

64 Bulloch and Morris: *Saddam's War*, p 26.

65 Darwish and Alexander: *The Secret History*, pp 228–9.

66 Darwish and Alexander: *The Secret History*, p 236.

67 Mohammed Heikal, *Illusions of Triumph*, p 135.

68 Uriel Dann, 'The Kurdish national movement in Iraq', *The Jerusalem Quarterly*, no. 9 (Fall, 1978) p 132.

69 Hanna Batatu: *The Old Social Classes*, p 1094.

70 Dann: 'The Kurdish national movement', p 142.

71 Amatzia Baram, *Culture, History, and Ideology in the Formation of Bathist Iraq: 1968–89* (New York, 1991) p 125.

72 Baram: *Culture, History and Ideology*, p 125.

73 Baram: *Culture, History and Ideology*, p 133.

74 Steven Bashkett, *Iraq and the Pursuit of Nonalignment*, p 480.

75 Bashkett: *Iraq*, p 483.

76 Saad al-Bazzaz, *Harb taled okhra: al-Tariq al-sirri li harb al-khalij* (Amman, 1992) p 49.

77 al-Bazzaz: *Harb taled okhra*, p 43.

78 al-Bazzaz: *Harb taled okhra*, pp 32–3.

79 al-Bazzaz: *Harb taled okhra*, p 50.

80 al-Bazzaz: *Harb taled okhra*, p 63.

81 Heikal: *Illusions of Triumph*, p 123.

82 Heikal: *Illusions of Triumph*, p 131.

Chapter 3 The State of Iraq

1 Quoted in Reeva S. Simon, *Iraq Between the Two World Wars: The Creation and Implementation of a Nationalist Ideology* (New York, 1986) p 1.

2 Quoted in Hanna Batatu, *The Old Social Classes and the Revolutionary Movements of Iraq: A Study of Iraq's Old Landed and Commercial Classes and of its Communists, Ba'thists, and Free Officers* (Princeton, 1978) pp 25–6.

3 Simon Henderson, *Instant Empire: Saddam Hussein's Ambition for Iraq* (San Francisco, 1991) p 1.

4 Henderson: *Instant Empire*, p 133.

5 Christine M. Helms, *Iraq, Eastern Flank of the Arab World* (Washington DC, 1984) p 8.

6 Ahmad Yusuf Ahmad, 'The dialectics of domestic environment and role performance: the foreign policy of Iraq', in Bahgat Korany and Ali E. Hillal Dessouki (eds), *The Foreign Policies of Arab States* (Boulder, 1984) p 149.

7 Helms: *Iraq: Eastern Flank*, p 10.

8 Helms: *Iraq: Eastern Flank*, pp 10–11.

9 Sa'ad Jawad, *Iraq and the Kurdish Question, 1958–1970* (London, 1981) p 229.

10 Amatzia Baram, *Culture, History, and Ideology in the Formation of Bathist Iraq, 1968–89* (New York, 1991).

11 Nader Entessar, *Kurdish Ethnonationalism* (Boulder, 1992) p 79.

12 Entessar: *Kurdish Ethnonationalism*, p 79.

13 Eberhard Kienle, *Ba'th v. Ba'th: The Conflict Between Syria and Iraq, 1968–1989* (London, 1990) p 2.

14 Kienle: *Ba'th v. Ba'th*, p 4.

15 Batatu: *The Old Social Classes*, p 1003.

16 Helms: *Iraq: Eastern Flank*, p 59.

17 Kamel S. Abu Jaber, *The Arab Ba'th Socialist Party: History, Ideology, and Organization* (Syracuse, 1966) p 139.

18 Abu Jaber: *The Arab Ba'th Socialist Party*, p 87.

19 Abu Jaber: *The Arab Ba'th Socialist Party*, pp 139–40.

20 Michael C. Hudson, *Arab Politics: the Search for Legitimacy* (New Haven, 1977) p 275.

21 Ofra Bengio, 'Saddam Hussein's quest for power and survival', *Asian and African Studies*, 15 (November 1981) pp 323–41.

22 Batatu: *The Old Social Classes*, p 1078.

23 Batatu: *The Old Social Classes*, p 1088.

24 Quoted in Munir Nasser, 'Iraq's ethnic minorities and their impact on politics', *Journal of South Asian and Middle Eastern Studies*, 8, no. 3 (Spring, 1985) pp 22–37.

25 Ofra Bengio, 'Ba'thi Iraq in search of identity: Between ideology and praxis', *Orient*, 28, no. 4 (1987) p 512.

26 Helms: *Iraq: Eastern Flank*, p 114.

27 For further information, see Helms: *Iraq: Eastern Flank*, Chapter 4.

28 Joe Stork, 'State power and economic structure: class determination and state formation in contemporary Iraq', in Tim Niblock (ed.), *Iraq: The Contemporary State* (London, 1982) p 32.

29 *OPEC Member Country Profiles*, published by the Secretariat of the Organization of the Petroleum Exporting Countries, p 52.

30 Stork: 'State power and economic structure', pp 41–4.

31 Stork: 'State power and economic structure', p 41.

32 Stork: 'State power and economic structure', p 39.

33 Charles Tripp, 'Domestic politics in Iraq: Saddam Hussein and the autocratic fallacy', in Anoushiravan Ehteshami, Gerd Nonneman and Charles Tripp (eds), *War and Peace in the Gulf: Domestic Politics and Regional Relations into the 1990s* (Exeter, 1991) pp 23–4.

34 Faleh Abd al Jabar, 'Roots of an adventure: the invasion of Kuwait, Iraqi political dynamics', in Victoria Brittain (ed.), *The Gulf Between Us* (London, 1991) p 34.

35 Abd al Jaber, 'Roots of an adventure', p 39.

36 Khalid Izzi, *The Shatt al-Arab Dispute: A Legal Study* (London, 1981) p 25.

37 Izzi: *The Shatt al-Arab Dispute*, p 27.

38 Miron Rezun, *Saddam Hussein's Gulf Wars: Ambivalent Stakes in the Middle East* (Westport, 1992) p 47.

39 Stephen C. Pelletier, *The Iran–Iraq War: Chaos in a Vacuum* (New York, 1992) p 9.

40 Rezun: *Saddam Hussein's Gulf Wars*, p 30.

41 Quoted in Johannes Reissner, 'The Iranian Revolution and the Iran–Iraq War', in Hanns Maull and Otto Pick (eds), *The Gulf War: Regional and International Dimensions* (London, 1989) p 61.

42 Majid Khadduri, *The Gulf War: The Origins and Implications of the Iraq–Iran Conflict* (Oxford, 1988) p 111.

43 Reissner: 'The Iranian Revolution', p 63.

44 Shahram Chubin, 'Iran and the war: from stalemate to ceasefire', in Efraim Karsh (ed.), *The Iran–Iraq War: Impact and Implications* (London, 1989) p 14.

45 Lawrence Freedman and Efraim Karsh, *The Gulf Conflict 1990–1991: Diplomacy and War in the New World Order* (London, 1993) p 22.

46 Yezid Sayigh, *Arab Military Industry, Capability, Performance and Impact* (London, 1992) pp 103–4.

47 This is based on the author's own calculations. By adding the allocation of defense in the countries mentioned above, as a percentage of their GDP in 1978, and comparing it to that of Iraq in the same period, the total was 20.6% while that of Iraq was 21%.

48 Freedman and Karsh: *The Gulf Conflict*, p 37.

49 Mofid: *The Economic Consequences of the Gulf War* (London, 1990) p 87.

50 Mofid: *Economic Consequences*, p 89.

51 Eugen Wirth, 'Irak am Vorabend des Uberfalls auf Kuwait: zur Wirtschaftlichen und Socialen Dynamik im Jahrzehnt des Golfkriegs 1980–1990', *Orient*, 31, 3 (1990) p 378.

52 Helen Chapin Metz (ed.), *Iraq: A Country Study* (Washington DC, Headquarters, Dept. of the Army, 1990) pp 123–4.

53 Abd al Jabar: 'Roots of an adventure', p 35.

54 Abd al Jabar: 'Roots of an adventure', p 33.

55 Freedman and Karsh: *The Gulf Conflict*, p 38.

56 Freedman and Karsh: *The Gulf Conflict*, p 39.

57 Saad al-Bazzaz, *Harb taled okhra: al-Tariq al-sirri li harb al-khalij* (Amman, 1992) p 29.

58 al-Bazzaz: *Harb taled okhra*, p 30.

59 al-Bazzaz: *Harb taled okhra*, p 32.

Chapter 4 The Gulf War

1 Ibrahim Ibrahim (ed.), *The Gulf Crisis: Background and Consequences* (Washington DC, 1992) p 6.

2 Ibrahim (ed.): *The Gulf Crisis*, pp 7–8.

3 For further details, see Mustafa M. Alani, *Operation Vantage: British Military Intervention in Kuwait, 1961* (Surbiton, 1990).

4 For further analysis, see Mohammed H. Heikal, *Illusions of Triumph: An Arab View of the Gulf War* (London, 1992).

5 Janice Gross Stein, 'The security dilemma in the Middle East', in Bahgat Korany, Paul Noble and Rex Brynen (eds), *The Many Faces of National Security in the Arab World* (London, 1993) p 59.

6 Stein: 'The security dilemma', p 60.

7 In the course of the public hearings on the Irangate scandal, it emerged that an agreement had been signed between the CIA and the Iraqi intelligence soon after the opening of the US embassy in Baghdad in 1982, for an exchange of information.

8 Lawrence Freedman and Efraim Karsh, *The Gulf Conflict, 1990–1991: Diplomacy and War in the New World Order* (Princeton, 1993) pp 27–8.

9 Simon Henderson, *Instant Empire: Saddam Hussein's Ambition for Iraq* (San Francisco, 1991) p 219.

10 Heikal: *Illusions of Triumph*, p 175.

11 Ofra Bengio (ed.), *Saddam Speaks on the Gulf Crisis: A Collection of Documents* (Tel Aviv, 1992) pp 93–4.

12 Saad al-Bazzaz, *Harb taled okhra: al-Tariq al-sirri li harb al-khalij* (Amman, 1992) p 43.

13 al-Bazzaz: *Harb taled okhra*, p 43.

14 Milton Viorst, 'Report from Baghdad', *The New Yorker*, 24 September 1990.

15 Stein: 'The security dilemma'.

16 Norman Friedman, *Desert Victory: The War for Kuwait* (Annapolis, MD: Naval Institute Press, 1991) p 32.

17 The transcript was released by the Iraqi authorities. The State Department neither confirmed nor denied it. Cited in Micah L. Sifry and Christopher Cerf (eds), *The Gulf War Reader: History, Documents, Opinions* (New York, 1991) pp 122–30.

18 Mustafa M. Alani, *Operation Vantage, British Military Intervention in Kuwait, 1961* (Surbiton, 1990) p 83.

19 Anoushiravan Ehteshami, Gerd Nonneman and Charles Tripp (eds), *War and Peace in the Gulf: Domestic Politics and Regional Relations in the 1990s* (Exeter, 1991) p 97.

20 Philip Robins, 'Iraq in the Gulf War: Objectives, strategies, and problems', in Hanns Maull and Otto Pick (eds), *The Gulf War: Regional and International Dimensions* (London, 1989) p 47.

21 Ursula Braun, 'The Gulf Cooperation Council', in Hans Maull and Otto Pick (eds), *The Gulf War: Regional and International Dimensions* (London, 1989) p 91.

22 Ehteshami, Nonneman and Tripp: *War and Peace in the Gulf*, p 111.

23 Braun: 'The Gulf Cooperation Council', p 92.

24 Anthony Cordesman, 'The Regional Balance', in Hans Maull and Otto Pick (eds), *The Gulf War: Regional and International Dimensions* (London, 1989) p 81.

25 Ehteshami, Nonneman and Tripp: *War and Peace in the Gulf*, p 108.

26 Braun: 'The Gulf Cooperation Council', p 96.

27 See *Time* magazine, 11 February 1991, pp 36–7.

28 Michael Walzer, 'Justice and injustice in the Gulf War', in David E. Decosse (ed.), *But Was It Just? Reflections on the Morality of the Persian Gulf War* (New York, 1992) p 8.

29 David Scheffer, 'Use of force after the Cold War: Panama, Iraq, and the New World Order', in Louis Henkin (ed.), *Right versus Might: International Law and the Use of Force* (New York, Council on Foreign Relations Press, 1991) p 127.

30 BBC World Service (compil.), *Gulf Crisis Chronology* (Essex, 1991) p 8.

31 BBC World Service: *Gulf Crisis Chronology*, p 22.

32 BBC World Service: *Gulf Crisis Chronology*, p 106.

33 *Time*, 11 February 1991, p 136.

34 William O'Brien, *The Conduct of Just and Limited War* (New York, 1981) pp 13–14.

35 Scheffer, 'Use of force', p 137.

36 Michael Walzer, 'Justice and injustice', p 9.

37 George Wiegel, 'From last resort to endgame: morality, the Gulf War, and the peace process', in David E. Decosse (ed.), *But Was It Just? Reflections on the Morality of the Persian Gulf War* (New York, 1992) p 23.

38 Wiegel: 'From last resort', p 7.

39 *La Civilta Cattolica*, quoted and translated by Peter Heinegg in 'Modern war and Christian conscience', in David E. Decosse (ed.), *But Was It Just? Reflections on the Morality of the Persian Gulf War* (New York, 1992) p 23.

40 *Time*, 11 February 1991, p 37.

41 'Crisis in the Persian Gulf Region: US Policy Options and Implications', United States Senate, One Hundred First Congress, Second Session (Washington, 1990), p 208.

42 *Washington Post*, 9 December 1990.

43 James Turner Johnson and George Wiegel, *Just War and the Gulf War* (Washington, 1991), p 26.

44 Anthony Clark Arend and Robert J. Beck, *International War and the Use of Force: Beyond the U.N. Charter Paradigm* (London and New York, 1993) p 52.

45 Wiliam O'Brian, *Law and Morality in Israel's War with the PLO* (New York, 1991) p 89.

Bibliography

Abd al Jabar, Faleh, 'Roots of an adventure: the invasion of Kuwait, Iraqi political dynamics', in Victoria Brittain (ed.), *The Gulf Between Us* (London, 1991), pp 27–41

Abrahamian, Ervand, *Radical Islam: The Iranian Mojahedin* (London, 1989)

Abu Jaber, Kamel, *The Arab Ba'th Socialist Party: History, Ideology, and Organization* (Syracuse, 1966)

Ahmad, Ahmad Yusuf, 'The dialectics of domestic environment and role performance: the foreign policy of Iraq' in Bahgat Korany and Ali E. Hillal Dessouki (eds), *The Foreign Policies of Arab States: The Challenge of Change* (Boulder, 1984; Oxford, 1991)

Alani, Mustafa M., *Operation Vantage: British Military Intervention in Kuwait, 1961* (Surbiton, 1990)

Allison, Graham, *Essence of Decision* (New York, 1971)

Almond, Gabriel, 'A developmental approach to political systems', *World Politics*, 17, no.2 (January 1965) pp 183–214

Almond, Gabriel, and Powell, Bingham, *Comparative Politics: A Development Approach* (Boston, 1966)

Almond, Gabriel and Verba, Sidney, *The Civic Culture: Political Attitudes and Democracy* (New York, 1963)

———, *The Civic Culture Revisited* (Newbury Park, 1989)

Anderson, Lisa, 'The state in the Middle East and North Africa', *Comparative Politics*, 19 (October 1987) pp 1–18

Aoudah, Boutrose, *The Gulf War: Who is Responsible?* (Amman, 1991)

Arend, Anthony Clark and Beck, Robert J., *International War and the Use of Force: Beyond the U.N. Charter Paradigm*, (London and New York, 1993)

Art, Robert and Jervis, Robert (eds), *International Politics: Anarchy, Force, Political Economy, and Decision Making* (New York, 1984)

Assiri, Abdul-Reda, *Kuwaiti Foreign Policy: City-State in World Politics* (Boulder, 1990)

Axelrod, Robert, *The Evolution of Co-operation* (New York, 1984)

Baram, Amatzia, *Culture, History, and Ideology in the Formation of Ba'thist Iraq 1968–89* (New York and Oxford, 1991)
———, 'Qawmiyya and wataniyya in Ba'thi Iraq: the search for a new balance', *Middle Eastern Studies*, 19, no. 2 (April 1983) pp 188–200
———, 'Mesopotamian identity in Ba'th Iraq', *Middle Eastern Studies*, 19, no. 4 (October 1983) pp 426–55
———, 'Saddam Hussein: a political profile', *The Jerusalem Quarterly*, no. 17 (Fall 1989) pp 115–44
Batatu, Hanna, *The Old Social Classes and the Revolutionary Movements of Iraq: A Study of Iraq's Old Landed and Commercial Classes and Its Communists, Ba'thists and Free Officers* (Princeton, 1978)
al-Bazzaz, Saad, *Harb taled okhra: al-Tariq al-sirri li harb al-khalij* (Amman, 1992)
Ben-Dor, Gabriel, *State and Conflict in the Middle East: Emergence of the Postcolonial State* (New York, 1983)
Bengio, Ofra, 'Saddam Hussein's quest for power and survival', *Asian and African Studies*, no. 15 (1981) pp 323–41
———, 'Ba'thi Iraq in search of identity: between ideology and praxis', *Orient* 28, no. 4 (1987) pp 511–18
———, (ed.), *Saddam Speaks on the Gulf Crisis: A Collection of Documents* (Tel Aviv, 1992)
Bienen, Henry (ed.), *The Military and Modernization* (Rockway Beach, NY, 1971).
Bill, James and Leiden, Carl, *Politics in the Middle East* (Boston, 1984)
Blainely, Geoffrey, *The Causes of War* (London, 1988)
Braun, Ursula, 'The Gulf Cooperation Council' in Hanns Maull and Otto Pick (eds), *The Gulf War: Regional and International Dimensions* (London, 1989), pp 90–102
Bresheeth, Haim, and Yuval-Davis, Nira (eds), *The Gulf War and the New World Order* (London, 1991)
Brittain, Victoria (ed.), *The Gulf Between Us: The Gulf War And Beyond* (London, 1991)
Brodie, Bernard, *War and Politics* (New York, 1973)
Bull, Hedley, *The Anarchical Society: A Study in Order in World Politics* (London, 1990)
Bulloch, John and Morris, Harvey, *Saddam's War: The Origins of the Kuwait Conflict and the International Response* (London, 1991)
Bullock, Alan, *Hitler and Stalin: Parallel Lives* (London, 1991)
Butterfield, Herbert, *History and Human Relations* (London, 1951)
Butterworth, Charles, 'State and authority in Arab political thought', in G. Salamé (ed.), *The Foundations of the Arab State* (New York, 1987)

Carr, Edward Hallett, *The Twenty Years' Crisis: 1919–1939* (New York, 1964)

Chubin, Shahram, 'Iran and the war: from stalemate to ceasefire', in Efraim Karsh (ed.), *The Iran–Iraq War: Impact and Implications* (London, 1989), pp 13–25

Cleveland, William L., *A History of the Modern Middle East* (Boulder, 1994)

Cobban, Alfred, *Dictatorship: Its History and Theory* (New York, 1971)

Cordesman, Anthony, *The Gulf and the West: Strategic Relations and Military Realities,* (Boulder, 1988)

———, 'The Regional Balance', in Hanns Maull and Otto Pick (eds), *The Gulf War: Regional and International Dimensions* (London, 1989)

———, *After The Storm: The Changing Military Balance in the Middle East* (London, 1993)

Coser, Lewis, *The Function of Social Conflict* (London, 1965)

Cox, Richard, *Locke on War and Peace* (Oxford, 1960)

Creighton, Colin and Shaw, Martin (eds), *The Sociology of War and Peace* (London, 1987)

Dann, Uriel, 'The Kurdish national movement in Iraq', *The Jerusalem Quarterly,* 9, Fall 1978.

Dannreuther, Roland, 'The Gulf Conflict: a political and strategic analysis' *Adelphi Papers,* no. 264 (Winter 1991/92)

Darwish, Adel and Alexander, Gregory, *The Secret History of Saddam's War: Unholy Babylon* (London, 1991)

Dawisha, Adeed and Zartman, William (eds), *Beyond Coercion: The Durability of the Arab State* (London, 1988)

Davies, Charles (ed.), *After the War: Iran, Iraq and the Arab Gulf* (Chichester, 1990)

Decosse, David E. (ed.), *But Was It Just? Reflections on the Morality of the Persian Gulf War* (New York, 1992)

Deutsch, Karl, 'Social mobilization and political development', *American Political Science Review,* 55, no. 3 (September 1961), pp 493–514

Devlin, John F., *The Ba'th Party: A History from its Origins to 1966* (Stanford, 1976)

Durbin, E. F. M. and Bowlby, J., *Personal Aggressiveness and War* (London, 1939)

Easton, David, 'An approach to the analysis of political system', *World Politics,* 9, no. 3 (April, 1957), pp 383–400

Ehteshami, Anoushiravan, Nonneman, Gerd and Tripp, Charles (eds), *War and Peace in the Gulf: Domestic Politics and Regional Relations in the 1990s* (London, 1991)

Einstein, Albert and Freud, Sigmund, 'Why war? Open letters between Einstein and Freud', *The New Commonwealth Pamplet,* no. 6 (January, 1934)

Eisenstadt, Shmuel Noah (ed.), *Max Weber on Charisma and Institution-Building: Selected Papers* (Chicago, 1968)

Elwes, R. H. M., *The Chief Works of Benedict de Spinoza*, Vol II (Dover, 1951)

Entessar, Nader, *Kurdish Ethnonationalism* (Boulder, 1992)

Erikson, Erik, *Childhood and Society* (London, 1984)

————, *Identity, Youth and Crisis* (London, 1968)

Eysenck, Hans Jurgen, 'War and aggressiveness: a survey of social attitudes', in Tom Hatherley Pear (ed.), *Psychological Factors in Peace and War* (London, 1950) pp 49–81

Fahmy, Ismael, *Negotiating for Peace in the Middle East* (Baltimore, 1983)

Feinberg, Richard, *The Intemperate Zone: The Third World Challenge to U.S. Foreign Policy* (Ontario, 1983)

Feshbach, Seymour, 'Psychology, human violence and the search for peace: issues in science and social values', *Journal of Social Issues*, 46, no. 1 (1990), pp 183–98

Forsyth, Murray, 'Thomas Hobbes and the external relations of states', *International Studies*, 5 (1979), pp 196–209

Freedman, Lawrence and Karsh, Efraim, *The Gulf Conflict 1990–1991: Diplomacy and War in the New World Order* (London and Princeton, 1993)

Freud, Sigmund, *Totem and Taboo* (London, 1957)

Friedman, Norman, *Desert Victory: The War for Kuwait* (Annapolis, 1991)

Galbraith, John Kenneth, *The Anatomy of Power* (Boston, 1983)

Gallie, W. B., 'Power politics and war cultures', *Review of International Studies*, 14 (1988)

Gerassi, John, (ed.) *Venceremos; The Speeches and Writings of Ernesto Che Guevara*, (London, 1968)

al-Ghazali, *On the Duties of Brotherhood*, trans. Muhtar Holland (London, 1975)

Gilpin, Robert, 'The global political system', in J. D. B. Miller (ed.), *Order and Violence: Hedley Bull and International Relations* (Oxford, 1990) pp 112–39

Gunn, John Charles, *Violence in Human Society* (Newton Abbott, 1973)

Halle, Louis H., *Political Realism and Political Idealism* (Chicago, 1951)

Heikal, Mohamed, *Illusions of Triumph: An Arab View of the Gulf War* (London, 1992)

Helms, Christine, *Iraq: Eastern Flank of the Arab World* (Washington DC, 1984)

Henderson, Simon, *Instant Empire: Saddam Hussein's Ambition for Iraq* (San Francisco, 1991)

Henry, Jule, *Culture Against Man* (Harmondsworth, 1972)

Hinnebusch, Raymond A., 'Syria under the Ba'th: state formation in a fragmented society', *Arab Studies Quarterly*, 4, no. 3 (Summer 1992), pp 100–102

Hiro, Dilip, *Desert Shield to Desert Storm: the Second Gulf War* (London, 1992)
———, *The Longest War: the Iran–Iraq Military Conflict* (London, 1990)

Hobbes, Thomas, *Leviathan* edited and with an introduction by C. B. Macpherson (Harmondsworth, 1981)

Hoffmann, Stanley, *The State of War: Essays on the Theory and Practice of International Politics* (New York, 1968)
———, 'The uses and limits of the international law', in Robert Art and Robert Jervis (eds), *International Politics: Anarchy, Force, Political Economy and Decision-making* (New York, 1984)

Howard, Michael, *The Causes of War* (Cambridge, Harvard University Press, 1984)

Hudson, Michael C., *Arab Politics: the Search for Legitimacy* (New Haven, 1977)

Huntington, Samuel P. (ed.), *Changing Patterns in Military Politics* (New York, 1962)
———, 'The clash of civilizations?' *Foreign Affairs* 72, no. 3 (Summer 1993), pp 22–49

Hussein, Saddam, *Saddam Hussein on Current Events in Iraq*, translated by Khalid Kishtainy (London, 1977)

Ibn Khaldun, *al-Muqaddimah* trans. Franz Rosenthal (Princeton, 1981)

Ibrahim, Ibrahim (ed.), *The Gulf Crisis: Background and Consequences* (Washington DC, 1992)

Iskandar, Amir, *Saddam Hussein: Munadilan, wa mufakiran, wa insanan* (Paris, 1981)
———, *Saddam Hussein: An Official Biography* (Paris, 1980)

Izzi, Khaled, *The Shatt Al-Arab Dispute, A Legal Study* (London, 1981)

Jawad, Sa'ad, *Iraq and the Kurdish Question, 1958–1970* (London, 1981)

Jervis, Robert, 'Cooperation under the security dilemma', *World Politics* 30, no. 2 (January 1978), pp 167–214
———, 'The spiral of international insecurity', in Richard Little and M. Smith (eds), *Perspectives on World Politics: A Reader* (London, 1991) pp 91–101

Johnson, James Turner and Wiegel, George, *Just War and the Gulf War* (Washington, 1991)

Karsh, Efraim (ed.), *The Iran–Iraq War: Impact and Implications* (London, 1989)

Karsh, Efraim and Rautsi, Inari, *Saddam Hussein: A Political Biography* (London, 1991)

Kegley, Charles and Raymond, Gregory, *When Trust Breaks Down: Alliance Norms and World Politics* (Columbia, University of South Carolina Press, 1990)

Kennan, George F., *Around the Cragged Hill: A Personal and Political Philosophy* (New York, 1993)

Keohane, Robert, *Neorealism and its Critics* (New York, 1986)

Kerr, Madelaine, 'Personality and attitude towards warfare', in Tom Hatherley Pear (ed.), *Psychological Factors in Peace and War* (London, 1950), pp 83–90

Khadduri, Majid, *Socialist Iraq: A Study in Iraqi Politics since 1968* (Washington DC, 1978)

———, *Arab Personalities in Politics* (Washington DC, 1981)

———, *The Gulf War: The Origins and Implications of the Iraq–Iran Conflict* (Oxford, 1988)

Khalidi, Walid, 'Thinking the unthinkable: a sovereign Palestinian state', *Foreign Affairs*, 56, no. 3 (July 1978) pp 695–713

al-Khalil, Samir, *Republic of Fear* (Berkeley, 1989; London, 1991)

Khoury, Philip and Kostiner, Joseph, (eds), *Tribes and State Formation in the Middle East* (London, 1991)

Kienle, Eberhard, *Ba'th v. Ba'th: The Conflict between Syria and Iraq, 1968–1989* (London, 1990)

Korany, Bahgat, and Dessouki, Ali E. Hillal (eds), *The Foreign Policies of Arab States: The Challenge of Change* (Oxford, 1991)

Landau, Jacob (ed.), *Man, State, and Society in the Contemporary Middle East* (New York, 1972)

Lapidus, Ira, 'Tribes and state formation in Islamic history' in Philip Khoury and Joseph Kostiner (eds), *Tribes and State Formation in the Middle East* (London, 1991), pp 25–47

Laslett, Peter (ed.), *Locke: Two Treatises of Government* (Cambridge, Cambridge University Press, 1970)

Lasswell, Harold Dwight, *Power and Personality* (New York, 1948)

———, *The Analysis of Political Behavior: An Empirical Approach* (London, 1951)

Lefever, Ernest W., 'Reining in the UN: mistaking the instrument for the actor', *Foreign Affairs*, 72, no. 3 (Summer 1993), pp 17–20

Levy, Jack, 'Domestic politics and war', *Journal of Interdisciplinary History*, 18, no. 4 (Spring 1988), pp 653–73

Lewis, Bernard, 'Loyalty to community, nation and state', in G. Wise and C. Issawi (eds), *Middle East Perspective: The Next Twenty Years* (Princeton, 1981)

Lewis, Bernard (ed.), *Islam: From the Prophet Muhammad to the Capture of Constantinople*, Vol. I (New York, 1974; London, 1976)

Lieber, Robert, *No Common Power* (New York, 1991)

———, *Theory and World Politics* (London, 1973)

———, 'Existential realism after the Cold War', *The Washington Quarterly* (Winter, 1993)

Little, Richard, 'The liberal hegemony and the realist assault: competing ideological theories of the state', in Michael Banks and Martin Shaw (eds), *State and Society in International Relations* (London, 1991) pp 19–38

Little, Richard and Smith, M. (eds), *Perspectives on World Politics: A Reader* (London, 1991)

Luciani, Giacomo (ed.), *The Arab State* (London, 1990)

Macpherson, Crawford Brough, *The Political Theory of Possessive Individualism: Hobbes to Locke* (Oxford, 1962)

Mansfield, Peter, *The Arabs* (London, 1992)

———, 'Saddam Husain's political thinking: the comparison with Nasser', in Tim Niblock (ed.), *The Contemporary State* (London, 1982), pp 62–73

Mansfield, Sue, *The Rites of War: An Analysis of Institutionalized Warfare* (London, 1991)

Marr, Phebe, *The Modern History of Iraq* (Oxford, 1985)

Matar, Fuad, *Saddam Hussein: The Man, the Cause, and the Future* (London, 1981)

———, *Saddam Hussein: al-Sirat al-dhatiya wa'l-hizbiyat wa uslub al-hukm wa Idarat al-asira' 1937–1980* (London, 1989)

Maull, Hanns and Pick, Otto (eds), *The Gulf War: Regional and International Dimensions* (London, 1989)

Meibar, Basheer, *Political Culture, Foreign Policy and Conflict: The Palestine Area Conflict System* (Westport, 1982)

Menon, N. C., *Mother of All Battles: Saddam's Folly* (Delhi, 1991)

Metz, Helen Chapin (ed.), *Iraq: a Country Study* (Washington, DC, Headquarters, Dept of the Army, 1990)

Miller, Judith, and Mylroie, Laurie, *Saddam Hussein and the Crisis in the Gulf* (New York, 1990)

Mofid, Kamran, *The Economic Consequences of The Gulf War* (London, 1990)

Montesquieu, Charles de Secondat, *The Spirit of Laws*, edited by David Wallace Carrithers (Berkeley, 1977)

Morgenthau, Hans J., *Scientific Man vs. Power Politics* (Chicago, 1946)

———, *Politics among Nations* (New York, 1973)

Moser, Paul (ed.), *Rationality in Action* (Cambridge University Press, 1990)

Nasr, Seyyed Hossein, *Islam and the Plight of Modern Man* (London, 1975)

Nasser, Munir, 'Iraq's ethnic minorities and their impact on politics', *Journal of South Asian and Middle Eastern Studies*, 8, no. 3 (Spring 1985), pp 22–37

Niblock, Tim (ed.), *Iraq: The Contemporary State* (London, 1982)

Nizam Al-Deen, Irfan, *The Gulf War and the Roots of the Arabs' Dilemma* (London, 1991)

Oakeshott, Michael (ed.), *Leviathan or the Matter, Form and Power of a Commonwealth Ecclesiastical and Civil by Thomas Hobbes* (Oxford, 1928)

O'Brien, William, *The Conduct of Just and Limited War* (New York, 1981)

——, *Law and Morality in Israel's War with the PLO* (New York, 1991)

Osgood, Robert, *Alliances and American Foreign Policy* (Baltimore, 1971)

Othman, Ali, *The Concept of Man in Islam in the Writing of Al-Ghazali* (Cairo, 1960)

Owen, Roger, *State Power and Politics in the Making of the Modern Middle East* (London, 1992)

Oye, Kenneth (ed.), *Cooperation Under Anarchy* (Princeton, 1986)

Paret, Peter, *Clausewitz and the State: The Man, His Theories, and His Time* (Princeton, 1985)

Pelletier, Stephen C., *The Iran–Iraq War: Chaos in a Vacuum* (New York, 1992)

Picard, Elizabeth, 'Arab military politics: from revolutionary plot to authoritarian state', in Adeed Islam Dawisha, and Ira William Zartman (eds), *Beyond Coercion: The Durability of the Arab State* (London, 1988) pp 116–46

Rabinovich, Itamar and Esman, Milton (eds), *Ethnicity, Pluralism, and the State in the Middle East* (New York, 1988)

Rapoport, Anatol, 'Prisoner's dilemma: recollections and observations', in A. Rapoport (ed.), *Game Theory As a Theory of Conflict Resolution* (Dodrecht, 1974), pp 17–34

Rajai, Mostapha and Philips, Kay, 'Governments and radical oppositions: the psychologies of system-supporting and system-challenging behavior', *Journal of International Affairs*, 40, no.2 (Winter/Spring 1987), pp 353–72

Rauch, Leo, *Hegel and the Human Spirit: A Translation of the Jena Lectures on the Philosophy of Spirit (1805–6) with Commentary* (Detroit, 1983)

Reich, Bernard, *Political Leaders of the Contemporary Middle East and North Africa: A Biographical Dictionary* (New York, 1990)

Reissner, Johannes, 'The Iranian Revolution and the Iran–Iraq War' in Hanns Maull and Otto Pick (eds), *The Gulf War: Regional and International Dimensions* (London, 1989) pp 60–72

Rezun, Miron, *Saddam Hussein's Gulf Wars: Ambivalent Stakes in the Middle East* (Westport, 1992)

Rich, Paul, *The Invasion of the Gulf* (Cambridge, Alborough Press, 1991)

Richards, Alan and Waterbury, John, *A Political Economy of the Middle East* (San Francisco, 1990)

Riker, William, *The Theory of Political Coalitions* (New Haven, 1962)

Robins, Philip, 'Iraq in the Gulf War: objectives, strategies and problems', in Hanns Maull and Otto Pick (eds), *The Gulf War: Regional and International Dimensions* (London, 1989) pp 45–59

Rothstein, Robert, *Alliance and Small Powers* (New York, 1968)

Rothenberg, Gunther E., 'The origins, causes, and extentions, of wars of the French Revolution and Napoleon', *Journal of Interdisciplinary History*, 18, no. 4 (Spring 1988), pp 771–93

Rousseau, Jean-Jaccques, *The Social Contract and Discourses*, translated and with an introduction by G. D. H. Cole (London, 1955)

Safran, Nadav, *Saudi Arabia: The Ceaseless Quest for Security* (Cambridge, Harvard University Press, 1985)

Salinger, Pierre, and Laurent, Eric, *Secret Dossier: The Hidden Agenda Behind the Gulf War* (New York, 1991)

Sayigh, Yezid, *Arab Military Industry, Capability, Performance and Impact* (London 1992)

Scheffer, David, 'Use of force after the Cold War: Panama, Iraq and the New World Order', in L. Henkin (ed.), *Right versus Might: International Law and the Use of Force* (New York, Council on Foreign Relations Press, 1991)

Schwarzkopf, H. Norman and Petre, Peter, *General H. Norman Schwarzkopf; The Autobiography: It Does Not Take A Hero* (London, 1992)

Sciolino, Elaine, *The Outlaw State* (New York, 1991)

Seal, Patrick, *Asad: The Struggle for Syria* (London, 1987)

Sharabi, Hisham and Ani, 'Impact of class and culture on social behavior: The feudal bourgeois family in Arab society', in N. Itzkowitz, and C. L. Brown (eds), *Psychological Dimensions of Near Eastern Studies* (Princeton, 1977) pp 240–56

Shaw, Martin and Creighton, Colin (eds), *The Sociology of Peace and War* (London, 1987)

Shaw, Martin (ed.), *War, State & Society* (London, 1984)

Sifry, Micah L. and Cerf, Christopher (eds), *The Gulf War Reader: History, Documents, Opinions* (New York, 1991)

Simmel, Georg, *Conflict and the Web of Group Affiliations*, translated by Kurt H. Wolff and Reinhard Bendix (New York, 1964)

Simon, Reeva, *Iraq Between the Two World Wars: The Creation and Implementation of a Nationalist Ideology* (New York, 1986)

Skocpol, T., Evans, P. and Rueschemeyer (eds), *Bringing the State Back In* (Cambridge, Cambridge University Press, 1985)

Snyder, Glenn H., 'The balance of power and the balance of terror', in Robert Art and Robert Jervis (eds), *International Politics: Anarchy, Force, Political Economy and Decision-making* (New York, 1984)

Snyder, Glenn H., 'The security dilemma in alliance politics', *World Politics*, 36, no. 4 (July, 1984) pp 461–95

Snyder, Glenn H. and Diesing, Paul, *Conflict Among Nations: Bargaining, Decision-making and System Structure in National Crisis* (Princeton, 1977)

Snyder, Jack, 'The new thinking about the new international system', in J. Snyder and R. Jervis (eds), *Coping with Complexity in the International System* (Boulder, 1993)

Spinoza, Benedictus de, *The Political Works: the Tractatus Theologico in part and the Tractatus Politicus in full*, edited and translated by A. G. Wernham (Oxford, 1958)

Stein, A., *Why Nations Co-operate: Circumstances and Choices in International Relations* (London, 1990)

Stein, Janice Gross, 'The security dilemma in the Middle East: a prognosis for the decade ahead', in Bahgat Korany, Paul Noble, and Rex Brynen (eds), *The Many Faces of National Security in the Arab World* (London, 1993) pp 56–75

——, 'Report from Baghdad', in *The New Yorker*, 29 September 1990

Stoll, Richard, 'System and state in international politics: a computer simulation of balancing in an anarchic world', *International Studies Quarterly* (1987)

Stork, Joe, 'State power and economic structure: class determination and state formation in contemporary Iraq', in Tim Niblock (ed.), *Iraq: The Contemporary State* (London, 1982)

Suganami, Hidemi, 'Bringing order to the causes of war debate', *Journal of International Studies*, no. 1 (1990) pp 19–35

Strauss, Leo, *Thoughts on Machiavelli* (Chicago, 1978)

Taylor, Michael, *The Possibility of Co-operation: Studies in Rationality and Social Change* (Cambridge, Cambridge University Press, 1987)

Thompson, W. Kenneth, 'The dilemma and antinomies of leadership', *Presidential Studies Quarterly*, 14, no. 1 (Winter, 1984), pp 35–42

Tilly, Charles, 'War making and state making as organized crime', *Bringing the State Back In* (Cambridge, Cambridge University Press, 1985)

Tilly, Charles (ed.), *The Formation of National States in Western Europe* (Princeton, 1975)

Tripp, Charles (ed.), 'Domestic politics in Iraq: Saddam Hussein and the autocratic fallacy', in A. Ehteshami, G. Nonneman and C. Tripp (eds), *War and Peace in the Gulf: Domestic Politics and Regional Relations in the 1990s* (Exeter, 1991)

Walsh, Maurice (ed.), *War and the Human Race* (London, 1971)

Walt, Stephen, *The Origin of Alliances* (Ithaca, 1987)

Waltz, Kenneth, *Man, the State, and War* (New York, 1959)

————, *Theory of International Politics* (New York, 1979)

————, 'The origins of war in neorealist theory', *Journal of Interdisciplinary History*, 18, no. 4 (Spring, 1988) pp 615–28

————, 'The anarchic orders and balance of power', in Robert Art and Robert Jervis (eds), *International Politics: Anarchy, Force, Political Economy and Decision-making* (New York, 1984)

Walzer, Michael, 'Justice and injustice in the Gulf War', in David E. Decosse (ed.), *But Was It Just? Reflections on the Morality of the Persian Gulf War* (New York, 1992)

Watt, William Montgomery, *The Formative Period of Islamic Thought* (Edinburgh, 1973)

Weiner, Myron, and Huntington, Samuel P. (eds), *Understanding Political Development: An Analytical Study* (Boston, 1987)

Wiegel, George, 'From last resort to endgame: morality, the Gulf War and the peace process', in David E. Decosse (ed.), *But Was It Just? Reflections on the Morality of the Persian Gulf War* (New York, 1992)

Wight, Martin, *Power Politics* (Leicester, 1978)

Wirth, Eugen, 'Irak am Vorabend des Ueberfalls auf Kuwait: zur wirtschaftlichen und Sozialen Dynamik im Jahrzehnt des Golfkriegs 1980–1990', *Orient*, 31, no. 3 (1990) pp 363–78

Woodward, Peter, *Nasser: Profile in Power* (London, 1992)

Woolf, Leonard, *The War for Peace* (London, 1940)

Wright, Quincy, *A Study of War* (Chicago, 1971)

Yaniv, Avner, *Dilemmas of Security: Politics, Strategy, and the Israeli Experience in Lebanon* (Oxford, 1987)

Zur, Ofer, 'The psychohistory of warfare: the co-evolution of culture, psyche and enemy', *Journal of Peace Research*, 24, no. 2 (1987), pp 125–34

Reports

Anarchy or Order: United Nations Annual Reports, 1982–1991, New York, United Nations, 1991.

Gulf Crisis Chronology, compiled by BBC World Service, Directory Publishers, 1991.

OPEC Member Country Profiles, published by the Secretariat of the Organisation of Petroleum Exporting Countries.

Saddam's Iraq: Revolution or Reaction?, a report by CARDI, (Committee Against Repression and for Democratic Rights in Iraq), London, Zed Books, 1986.

Index